Housing Research F

Racial Attacks and Harassment: the Response of Social Landlords

Yvonne Dhooge and Jill Barelli
London Research Centre

London: HMSO
Department of the Environment

ISBN 0 11 753200 2

Recycled Paper

Contents

Page No.

Acknowledgements   vii

PART 1:   A REVIEW OF GOOD PRACTICE   1

1   General comments   3

2   Responding to racial harassment in social housing   8

3   Staff training   12

4   Racial harassment and housing allocations   13

5   Tenancy clauses forbidding harassment   15

6   Tenants' and residents' associations   16

7   Monitoring and evaluation   18

8   Households in temporary accommodation   20

9   The private sector   22

10   Racial harassment and the law   23

11   Competitive tendering of housing management   29

PART 2:   RESEARCH REPORT   31

12   Summary and conclusions   33
     Aims   33
     Method   33
     Response   33
     Policies on racial harassment   33
     Changes in local authorities since 1991   33
     Local authorities compared with housing associations   34
     Perpetrators   34

Tenants' associations and community groups   34

Multi-agency groups   34

Suggestions for improving practice   34

13   Introduction and background to the study   37

Research method   39

Response   39

14   Racial incidents recorded by social landlords   41

Sources of information   41

Racial harassment in the housing stock of respondents who did not complete the full questionnaire   42

Racial harassment in the housing stock of respondents to the full questionnaire   44

15   Policies on racial harassment   49

Tenure categories covered by policies and procedures on racial harassment   49

Ethnic records   51

Prevention of racial harassment   52

16   Working with other agencies   57

Providing information to others   57

Receiving information   59

Obstacles to sharing information   62

Multi-agency groups   63

Involvement in multi-agency working   63

How landlords are represented   64

Activities   65

The benefits of multi-agency working   65

Problems with multi-agency working   66

Conclusion   68

17   Supporting those experiencing harassment   69

Communication with potential victims   71

Improving organisational responses   71

Successes in helping victims   71

18   Dealing with perpetrators   73

Background   73

Action taken by landlords   74

Possession proceedings   75

Interviewing perpetrators   77

Other work with perpetrators   78
Working with other agencies   78
Attitudes of the courts   79
Communicating success   79

19   Carrying out surveys   81
Existence of local surveys   81
Use of survey findings   81
Need for survey advice   82
Other feedback methods   82

References   83

Annex 1   Fieldwork   85

Annex 2   Questionnaire   89

Acknowledgements

Yvonne Dhooge died of cancer in February 1996. We worked together on this project from the beginning and Yvonne completed several chapters of the report (and much else besides) during a period of great pain and anxiety. None of us who worked with her will ever forget her warmth, enthusiasm and courage.

Yvonne valued diversity and gave her time generously when approached for help with surveys about racism or the needs of minority groups. Many of the respondents to our questionnaire and the people who commented on the good practice guidelines showed a similar commitment, and I would like to thank them all.

Keith Kirby and Juliet Mountford managed the research on behalf of the DoE and contributed much encouragement, help and advice.

I would also like to thank Val White at the LRC for her support and her astute comments on the final draft.

Part 1   A review of good practice

The purpose of this review is to summarise recommended practice for social housing organisations and refer readers to sources of further information. A number of good practice guides have been written over the last 15 years, some of which (including DoE guidance published in 1989) are no longer in print. It may therefore be useful to provide an overview at this point.

There were people from ethnic minority groups living in every English local authority area at the time of the 1991 Census. Local authorities and the Housing Corporation have a legal duty to eliminate unlawful discrimination and promote equality of opportunity and good race relations. The general comments in chapter 1 therefore emphasise that social landlords in all areas should have a policy on the housing implications of racial attacks and harassment and be prepared to work with other organisations.

Landlords need to plan how they will respond if any of their own tenants are affected by harassment – this is covered in chapter 2. Chapter 3-7 provide further advice on staff training, allocations, tenancy clauses, tenants'/residents' associations, and monitoring and evaluation. Chapter 8 deals with households in temporary accommodation and chapter 9 with the private sector. Finally, there is a brief guide to the law in this area (chapter 10) and the implications of the competitive tendering of housing management (chapter 11). Social housing management organisations as well as landlords. All types of manger should be brought into any multi-agency arrangements, and their effectiveness in dealing with racial harassment should be monitored.

1 General comments

Racial attacks and harassment can take very many forms – verbal abuse, criminal damage, malicious complaints, graffiti, arson and murder can all be racially motivated. Black people and people from ethnic minorities are most at risk, but white people with black partners or mixed race children may also be targeted. An incident that might seem minor if the complainant or their property were selected at random takes on a different dimension if they have been targeted for a racial reason. The perpetrators of such crimes intend to victimise, and they often rely on the apathy or collusion of others.

The definitions of a racial incident and of racial harassment used by the police and by the Commission for Racial Equality (see paragraphs 16.41-16.43 of the research report in Part 2) emphasise how important it is to take into account the views of victims or other witnesses about the motivation of their attackers.

It is not just an issue for landlords operating in areas with significant ethnic minority populations. An isolated black tenant in an overwhelmingly white area is potentially in a very vulnerable position. The experience of racial harassment is made worse if social landlords fail to recognise and respond to the situation. Local authorities and housing associations who rarely or never receive complaints of racial harassment might wish take the following steps:

- develop an outline policy and procedure: who will do what if the need arises;

- obtain the guides recommended here and use them to plan their response;

- decide in advance where they will obtain legal advice, interpreters and victim support, because when the time comes these services may be needed in a hurry;

- check that newly housed black or ethnic minority tenants are not experiencing any problems;

- be alert for indirect signs of racial harassment (eg unexpected transfer or repair requests, or refusal of popular areas);

- make sure there is an anti harassment clause in tenancy agreements;

- have an arrangement in place with other authorities or associations in the area to assist with temporary or permanent rehousing on a reciprocal basis.

Although Pendle BC has relatively few ethnic minority tenants, the authority is represented on the local multi-agency forum and takes part in campaigns to raise awareness of racial harassment. There is a clause in the tenancy agreement, the racial origin of tenants is monitored and training is provided for senior managers.

Policy development should not be confined to social housing tenancies. Local housing authorities have strategic responsibility for privately rented and owner occupied housing, and should consider their role in addressing racial harassment in these sectors. Housing associations are important providers of shared ownership housing and manage an increasing number of privately rented properties. Both types of organisation assist homeless and vulnerable people, many of whom occupy accommodation on non secure tenancies and licences, sometimes in non-self contained accommodation such as hostels or bed and breakfast hotels.

The causes and effects of racial harassment extend beyond the housing management remit. Involve other agencies and service providers as appropriate and respond to their requests for help. Housing is not the only local authority department with a role to play in combating racial harassment, and it may be useful to have a written agreement which clearly sets out the responsibilities of (say) education, social services, legal, planning, environmental health and chief executive's. A similar approach could be agreed with outside agencies such as the police, racial equality councils, victim support, advice agencies and monitoring groups. In some areas, shared but clearly delineated responsibilities may already have been achieved through multi-agency working and/or contractual arrangements. The CRE's caseworkers handbook (see below) outlines the roles and responsibilities of a number of agencies, and its guide for multi-agency panels provides advice on setting up formal multi-agency arrangements.

In LB Hillingdon, the supported housing team (which includes other partners in providing community care such as health and social services) is investigating the incidence of racial or other forms of harassment experienced or perpetrated by people who are suffering from a mental illness, and how the landlord should respond and manage this.

Make the most of existing and potential resources. Tackling racial harassment requires time and money, but often as part of the wider service – eg remedying design defects helps prevents crime generally, including that element which is racially motivated. Similarly, it is not always necessary to invent new procedures when there is an existing procedure that can be adapted (eg for repairs, transfers). Some social landlords have provided access to community alarm systems for people at risk of racial harassment by linking them to systems already in place for elderly residents.

Be clear where racial harassment fits into wider housing policy. Social housing organisations should examine the relationship between their policies and procedures on racial harassment, and any policies they may have for dealing with nuisance, anti social behaviour or neighbour disputes. All forms of harassment call for a response, whether or not the motivation of perpetrators is apparent to those experiencing the harassment. Elements of good practice and specialist skills developed in one area may be applicable in another. A degree of consolidation may be desirable in order to provide a consistent level of service. Nevertheless, it is vital that racial motivation is recognised and addressed when it is encountered. The risk of repeat attacks is particularly high, others may join in or collude with the harassment, and preventative strategies have little chance of success unless they include attempts to challenge racism.

Always be prepared to take some action – if the perpetrators are children, or cannot be identified, it is still worth investigating the incidents and taking preventative measures – eg contacting parents, involving local schools.

People living on estates with severe housing and social problems sometimes blame minority groups for their predicament. Community development on such estates can help to produce a much more constructive response, especially if resources can be found to improve the area for everyone.

Tackling racial violence and harassment requires the following:

- commitment (at all levels);
- two plans: how to respond to racial harassment and how to try and prevent it;
- some resources (eg for security measures, legal services, publicity material);
- staff who have been trained and are clear about their responsibilities (see Section 3);
- access to expert advice/services should the need arise (eg legal, technical, interpreters, counselling);
- tenant and community involvement;
- systems for monitoring incidents and evaluating the response;
- a policy review process.

1a Sources of general advice on dealing with racial harassment

Eliminating Racial Harassment: a Guide to Housing Policies and Procedures, Richard Seager and Joanna Jeffery, Lemos Associates (now Lemos and Crane), 1994. 20 Pond Square, London N6 6BA, 0181 348 8263. A comprehensive guide that includes, for example:

- the pros and cons of various definitions;
- a model clause for tenancy agreements;
- good practice in interviewing victims;
- dealing with vulnerable perpetrators;
- administrative procedures and keeping records;
- advice on training;
- specimen forms for: initial reports, interviews with complainants, follow up;
- specimen diary form;
- specimen letters to tenants (where perpetrators unknown) and to the police;
- outline training programmes;
- terms of reference for a working party or panel on racial harassment.

Racial Harassment: Policies and Procedures for Housing Associations, NFHA, 1989. Includes:

- action list for housing association committees;
- model tenancy clause and procedure;
- specimen forms for: initial report, visits, witness report, repairs, follow up, previous incidents and personal record for further incidents.

Tackling Racial Harassment: a caseworker's handbook, CRE, 1995. Although this is written for people in advice agencies, housing staff may find some of the information and suggestions useful. It includes advice on:

- interviewing clients who are experiencing racial harassment and acting as their advocates;
- the role of other agencies (multi-agency panels, police, Crown Prosecution Service, housing providers, schools/local education authorities, health services, social services, employers);
- a summary of criminal and civil law;
- interview and incident report forms.

Action on Racial Harassment: a guide for multi-agency panels, CRE, 1995. This provides practical advice on establishing multi-agency panels in areas where they do not yet exist, and guidelines against which existing panels can examine their procedures and practices. It emphasises, however, that there is no 'right' formula – much depends on local circumstances. Includes:

- a list of the agencies that might become full or associate members, and advice on getting them involved;
- arrangements for co-ordinating casework;
- frameworks for policy development;
- a new recommended definition of racial harassment;
- advice on the classification of ethnic origin;
- guidelines for monitoring and evaluation.

Neighbour Nuisance: Ending the Nightmare, Good Practice Briefing Issue 3, CIH, 1995. This covers nuisance, anti social behaviour and harassment (all of which are defined) and includes numerous examples of LA and HA initiatives. Topics include:

- preventative measures;
- tenancy agreements;

- victim support and witness evidence;
- legal remedies and powers;
- mediation;
- working with the police.

Housing Management Standards Manual (section 11: equal opportunities), Chartered Institute of Housing. The 1995 edition includes:

- a summary of legal remedies in England and Wales, and Scotland;
- sample tenancy clauses;
- examples of victim support.

2   Responding to racial harassment in social housing

General guidelines

- Have a clear written policy, including a definition of racial harassment.
- Allocate responsibility for implementation to a senior officer (eg second tier).
- Provide training for staff at all levels – plus refresher and induction courses.
- Prepare written procedures that explain exactly who is responsible for doing what.
- Adopt a corporate approach across LA departments.
- Co-ordinate with other housing authorities/housing associations.
- Adopt a positive approach to multi-agency work.
- Maintain close liaison with experienced lawyers.
- Brief elected members and senior managers to support and explain the policy.
- Make arrangements for emergency access to interpreters, legal advice and victim support.

Responding to incidents

- Interview complainant and arrange practical support as soon as possible.
- Believe them until and unless there is clear evidence to the contrary.
- Seek agreement to involve the police/other agencies.
- Explain the options and discuss measures to support the complainant and action that might be taken against perpetrators. Do not proceed against the complainant's wishes[1].
- Back this up with written advice/support pack and an agreed action plan.
- Use standard report forms that meet the landlord's own information requirements and (as far as possible) those of other agencies with whom they may be working.
- Stay in touch and check if there have been further incidents (this still applies if a complainant is subsequently transferred).
- Protect the confidentiality of complainants (except where they have agreed that details should be passed to other agencies).
- Keep records in a secure place (this is also necessary for evidence purposes).
- Ask victims for their views on the service provided.

---

[1] Some organisations make an exception here if they feel the safety of others is at stake – eg through the risk of an arson attack.

- Always arrange for communication in an appropriate language.
- Photograph damage.
- Implement repairs and agreed security measures to a strict deadline.
- Remove graffiti within 24 hours.

Options for practical support

- Security measures – doors, windows, lighting, fences, fireproof letterboxes, video cameras, closed circuit TV, smoke and burglar alarms, security patrols (a code of practice on the use of surveillance equipment is desirable, covering, for example, consultation with residents and access to tapes. Local authorities are required by law to consult with the police before installing CCTV).
- Temporary rehousing (this might be required in the immediate aftermath of an attack, or around the time that witnesses are giving evidence in court).
- Personal alarms or mobile phones.
- 24 hour helpline.
- Emotional support or counselling (for example, putting people in touch with victim support, voluntary agencies or self help groups).
- Escorts (eg to school, work, shops) – some social landlords arrange for community groups, sympathetic neighbours or other volunteers to assist with this.

Dealing with perpetrators

- If there is a likelihood of criminal proceedings, the police may wish to take the lead in interviewing perpetrators.
- In other cases, social landlords should use the guide recommended below when interviewing alleged perpetrators who are tenants.
- Liaise with the police, local authority or housing association as appropriate about other perpetrators. An interview is still desirable – the LA or HA concerned may wish to be involved if the perpetrator is their tenant.
- Obtain advice at an early stage if it looks as if legal action may be required.
- Gather a high standard of evidence – liaise with the police and consider the use of surveillance equipment, professional witnesses and private investigators if necessary.
- Some complainants may be willing to keep a diary and take photographic evidence.
- Be prepared to use verbal and written warnings and to charge perpetrators for damage. Seek an injunction, prosecution or eviction if necessary – but be guided by the complainant's wishes. Some form of conciliation or mediation procedure may occasionally be appropriate.
- Injunctions may help to protect those experiencing harassment whilst possession proceedings are taking their course – but be prepared for the fact that some perpetrators have no respect for the law.

- Witnesses may need support and protection before, during and after any court proceedings, if necessary on a 24 hour basis. In some areas, volunteers have been drawn from local community groups or council staff when the police have been unable to assist.

- Perpetrators evicted for racial harassment may approach Homeless Persons Units. LAs and HAs should inform HPUs about evictions for racial harassment so that every such case can be examined carefully for evidence of intentional homelessness.

- If perpetrators are unknown, consider a more general warning letter; surveillance; preventative work; involvement of tenants' association. Liaise with the police to see if they would be willing to visit local residents and increase their presence in the area.

Prevention of racial violence and harassment

- Work with tenants' and residents' associations (see below).

- Community development work – eg provision of play facilities and youth activities, development of tenants'/residents' associations, self help groups.

- Educational initiatives in local schools and colleges.

- Publicity campaigns can be used to:

   a) encourage victims to come forward;

   b) influence the behaviour of people who might otherwise collude with the harassment;

   c) warn potential perpetrators of the consequences of their actions.

   If possible, campaigns should be repeated at regular intervals.

- Ensure that racial harassment is covered by the tenancy agreement (see below).

- Communicate the policy to potential complainants and perpetrators – use tenants' handbooks, newsletters, annual reports, conferences/public enquiries, local media, leaflets, videos, posters.

- Monitor the geographical pattern of reported incidents, vandalism, graffiti, transfer requests, preferences and refusals; and local events (eg involving racist political groups).

- Identify any particular properties that are vulnerable.

- Consider improvements to design and security on the worst affected estates.

- Liaise with the police on crime prevention initiatives.

- Include measures to improve security/combat harassment in planned maintenance and rehabilitation programmes and in bids for funding. Leicester CC, for example, obtained Safer Cities funding for video surveillance on an estate with a high incidence of racial harassment.

Finally

- Monitor and evaluate the response to racial harassment (see below).

- Assess the implications for allocations policies (see below).

- Share expertise and resources with other agencies; develop joint initiatives.

2a Further advice on dealing with perpetrators

Interviewing perpetrators requires a degree of preparation and skill. Every case is different and a rigid format can be counter productive. The feelings of interviewers may interfere with their ability to communicate clearly. But a well conducted interview can have positive outcomes: the harassment may stop; or it may be possible to obtain evidence that can be used in legal proceedings.

The central premise of Gerard Lemos' book **Interviewing Perpetrators of Racial Harassment: A Guide for Housing Managers** (Lemos Associates, 1993) is that 'most cases of racial harassment will ideally be resolved by stopping the harassment and maintaining the existing tenancies of both the victim and the perpetrator, not by moving one or the other, voluntarily or involuntarily.'

Includes advice on:

- how to prepare for and structure an interview;
- six common reactions on the part of perpetrators and how to respond.
- dealing with the emotions of those involved.
- proformas for recording information, action, questions and responses.
- what should happen after the interview.

Staff in housing organisations with little or no experience of dealing with perpetrators might find it extremely helpful to have this book to hand, since it will provide very practical and immediate advice.

3   Staff training

Everyone who might come into contact with victims or perpetrators (this includes receptionists, caretakers, wardens, housing advice and HPU staff, committee members and councillors) needs to have a clear understanding of what the racial harassment policy means and how it applies to their own role. Staff training is one of the best ways of imparting such an understanding.

Specific skills required for a narrower range of staff include interviewing (victims, other witnesses and alleged perpetrators) and collecting evidence. A working knowledge of legal remedies is also useful, although this does not obviate the need for professional advice. Training can also be used to impart confidence: people may be anxious about their own ability to handle such an emotive issue.

It may be appropriate to involve tenants and residents associations, voluntary organisations, community groups or the police in staff training sessions. The exchange of views and ideas can develop mutual understanding and lead to joint initiatives.

Refresher courses can be used to obtain feedback from staff on any problems or suggested improvements in service delivery, and to review any successes or failures.

4 Racial harassment and housing allocations

When housing applicants are able to express geographical preferences, black and ethnic minority applicants may avoid areas with a history of racial harassment, even when the housing is of high quality. People made offers of estates or individual properties with a recent history of attacks will often turn them down. One of the many costs of failing to tackle racial harassment is that allocations begin to appear discriminatory.

Transferring people experiencing harassment

The research in Part 2 shows that many social landlords view the transfer of the victim as a defeat. This attitude is understandable, since it appears to hand victory to the perpetrator, makes it more difficult to rehouse black and ethnic minority applicants in the area, and reinforces the belief of those who think that black tenants falsely claim racial harassment in order to obtain a transfer. Nevertheless, the risk and the stress associated with continuing in occupation sometimes makes a transfer unavoidable. It is not a failing to assist people in these circumstances. Moreover, transferring the victim does not preclude further action against perpetrators and preventative work in the area. Urgent management transfers, once agreed, should be effected as quickly as possible – preferably to a deadline.

Social rented tenants who are forced to seek a transfer through racial harassment may move to a property that is of poorer quality or less convenient for work, school, or community facilities. They will certainly incur removal expenses. Landlords may wish to consider what they can do to reduce this burden – eg by trying to find a property of similar quality, and by paying removal costs. Sandwell BC, for example, pays a discretionary disturbance allowance to cover removal/ reconnection expenses (this policy also applies to witnesses who fear reprisals for giving evidence).

Social landlords with small, localised housing stocks will sometimes need to make use of reciprocal arrangements with other authorities or associations in order to obtain suitable accommodation for people experiencing harassment. Procedures under the HOMES scheme can also be accelerated: for example, London boroughs have a 'fast track' arrangement that can be used in these circumstances.

Transferring perpetrators

Some tenant perpetrators are vulnerable (eg through mental illness) or they may live in households with others who are vulnerable. In such circumstances, it is occasionally necessary to rehouse perpetrators, by management transfer (with their agreement) or by obtaining possession subject to an offer of alternative accommodation. Alternative accommodation will need to be selected (as far as possible) to reduce the risk of further problems.

Reletting properties

Social landlords should be open with housing applicants if racially motivated crimes have taken place in a particular area and should not treat refusal of such properties as unreasonable. The only real solution to this problem is to put in the more difficult and time consuming work of dealing with perpetrators and changing the climate on the estate. People will be much more willing to accept an offer when they can be assured that the cause has been dealt with. Those who do accept offers of accommodation where there is a possibility of continuing harassment should be given practical support (eg security improvements, and contact with community groups or neighbours who would be willing to assist and provide support). Richard Seager and Joanna Jeffery provide further guidelines on the letting of vacated properties in *Eliminating Racial Harassment*.

When housing black or ethnic minority tenants on a previously all white estate, it is a sensible precaution for locally based staff to check (preferably as part of a routine visit) that they are not experiencing any problems.

Some tenant/property matches in areas with a recent history of harassment can produce vulnerable combinations – eg letting a corner property or one near a pub to a black lone parent or a disabled person. Notwithstanding the need to safeguard fairness in the allocations system, it may be advisable to avoid such lettings.

5 Tenancy clauses forbidding harassment

An express clause in the tenancy agreement serves to alert potential perpetrators to the landlord's policy on racial or other forms of harassment and to reassure potential victims. It may also strengthen the landlord's case in any possession proceedings and make it easier to obtain injunctions.

Several examples of 'no harassment' clauses currently in use are given in the *Housing Management Standards Manual*. Local authorities and housing associations are of course required to consult with secure tenants before introducing new clauses to their tenancy agreement. Housing associations wishing to vary the terms of an existing assured tenancy must obtain the express agreement of each tenant.

Anti harassment clauses should be worded carefully in order to make sure that they cover the actions of children and visitors as well as tenants themselves; and also to ensure that they can be used to protect the family and visitors of other tenants – not just the perpetrator's immediate neighbours. Richard Seager and Joanna Jeffery provide an example of such a clause in *Eliminating Racial Harassment*. In the case of assured tenancies, the NFHA model tenancy agreement contains a 'no harassment' clause. The pros and cons of different clauses are also discussed in the books recommended in Section 10a below.

Unfortunately, a form of words chosen to be legally watertight may conflict with the requirements of clear English. The clause should therefore be explained to people when they sign up for a tenancy, and in tenancy handbooks and newsletters.

There is a provision in the Housing Bill currently before Parliament which will, if enacted, broaden the statutory ground of possession for nuisance to include the behaviour of visitors (see also chapter 10). This will overcome a problem that many tenancy clauses have been designed to remedy. Express tenancy clauses will still be useful, however, because the Bill will also make it possible to attach a power of arrest to injunctions obtained by social landlords against a breach of tenancy.

6   Tenants' and residents' associations

The research in Part 2 suggests that local authorities and housing associations are doing comparatively little work with tenants' groups in order to try to prevent racial harassment. Tenants who are prepared to support people experiencing harassment, make witness statements and help isolate perpetrators can make an enormous difference. Tenants' associations can promote awareness of equal opportunities and harassment issues amongst tenants and alert landlords to local problems. A two way exchange of information on racial incidents should be encouraged, provided this does not contravene the wishes of those experiencing harassment.

TA members can be given advice and training with a view to developing their own policies on racial harassment and opening up participation in their association to black and ethnic minority tenants. Several local authorities provide training to tenants' and residents' associations on request – in Lambeth this covers the identification of racial harassment, the impact on those experiencing it, sources of support, and local authority legal obligations and policy.

Recognition and funding of formally constituted TAs, residents' associations and tenant management organisations should depend on a constitution which commits them to promote equal opportunities and combat harassment and discrimination. This is one of the recommended housing management standards of the Chartered Institute of Housing.

6a   Sources of advice on tenants' and residents' associations

All Together Now: involving black tenants in housing management, Joanna Jeffrey and Richard Seager, Tenant Participation Advisory Service, 1995. TPAS, Brunswick House, Broad Street, Salford M6 5BZ, 0161 745 7903. Written for local authorities and others who take on the management of council housing. Includes:

- consultation (including surveys) and participation arrangements (including reference to the introduction of housing management CCT);
- networking and support for the development of black and ethnic minority based organisations;
- good practice for tenant management organisations;
- recognition criteria for TAs;
- monitoring performance.

Getting Black Tenants Involved: a good practice guide for housing associations and co-operatives, Vernon Clarke, CATCH (Co-operative and Tenant Controlled Housing), 1994. (Copies can be obtained from Circle 33 Housing Association, telephone 0171 607 4727). Many of the suggestions in this guide are also relevant to local authorities and would be applicable in other contexts – eg involving black and ethnic minority groups in multi-agency work. Includes:

- barriers to communication and how to overcome them;
- examples of successful community development work;
- identifying and obtaining the resources needed to improve participation;
- checklist covering training, networking and the provision of information.

Room for All: Tenants' Associations and Racial Equality, Commission for Racial Equality, 1993. Includes:

- performance standards for landlords;
- an action plan for tenants' associations;
- a model constitution for TAs;
- a model equal opportunity statement;
- model conditions of recognition;
- model annual monitoring form.

7　Monitoring and evaluation

This should cover:

- reported incidents (although some agencies prefer to keep records on a household basis);

- any indirect indicators that are causing concern (repair and transfer requests; applicant preferences and refusal of properties);

- the response to individual cases – has contact been maintained with the complainant? Have any promises (eg in respect of security improvements) been met? Is action proceeding against identified perpetrators? Have there been any further incidents? Are urgent transfer applications receiving offers?

- an evaluation of policy and procedures.

For multi-agency panels, the CRE recommends self-classification of victims' ethnic origin and third party classification of perpetrators. It suggests that self-classification should be based on the ethnic groups used in the Census, but with 'Irish' identified as a sub-category of 'white'. For third party classification, it recommends the 'four plus one' code used by the police: white, black, Asian, other, and unknown.

Options to consider in areas with a regular throughput of cases:

- Separate the monitoring of the incidence and pattern of racial harassment from monitoring of the response (the two types of information serve rather different purposes). What is the profile of victims and perpetrators? Which estates and types of property are most affected? Are there particular times of the day or year? Are people seeking help from other local agencies?

- Have a clear system for tracking individual cases, but try to ensure that reporting arrangements can deliver more than this: ideally, individual cases should be collated so as to indicate the overall level of response (repairs, perpetrator interviews, transfers, installation of security alarms, legal moves etc) and performance against deadlines. Try to develop specific performance measures.

- Seek the views of those experiencing harassment about the service provided and incorporate these in monitoring reports and policy reviews. Also get feedback from the staff involved in implementing the policy: can procedures be improved?

- Remember, however, that the procedures are there to support victims and stop the harassment. They are not an end in themselves. Try to assess the extent to which they have helped those experiencing harassment and deterred further incidents.

- Be clear about agreements to share information with other agencies: is this to be done on a case by case or statistical basis? Is it to cover the response of each agency or just the nature and pattern of incidents? Is the purpose to prompt immediate action in individual cases (eg victim support or security measures); to assist with investigations; to promote longer term action (education campaigns, community development) or to facilitate evaluation of policies and procedures? The answers to these questions should determine the nature and timing of information exchange and the purpose and format of meetings.

- Sharing information (with the permission of complainants) is likely to be facilitated by the use of common incident forms and reporting systems. In Leeds, for example, a common report form is used by all agencies except the police (who collect more detailed information). The data is collated by Leeds City Council Equal Opportunities Unit for presentation to the multi-agency forum. In Southwark, common reporting forms have been developed for use by both voluntary and statutory agencies, including the police. Quarterly reports of aggregated information are distributed to all the participating agencies.

Monitoring in LB Waltham Forest

- Casework reviewed six weekly and used to develop action plan.

- Quarterly collation of statistics on number/type of incidents.

- Six monthly reports to Housing Committee – used in conjunction with other reports to develop policy (eg in respect of safety on estates).

- Questionnaire in victim support pack used to get feedback on client satisfaction. Findings reported to Housing Committee and used to evaluate need for additional training etc.

- Central monitoring, with statistics for each council department.

---

8   Households in temporary accommodation

Where households occupy accommodation on an assured shorthold tenancy or a licence, repossession procedures are usually simpler and quicker. This can make it easier to take action against perpetrators – but investigation of the circumstances should be no less thorough.

The Chartered Institute of Housing recommends in its *Housing Management Standards Manual* that compliance with harassment policies should be a condition of contracts with managing agents and with suppliers of temporary accommodation. They should also be required to provide monitoring reports of any such incidents occurring in accommodation they manage on behalf of social landlords.

Hostels and bed and breakfast hotels

Here the potential perpetrators could be staff or other residents – 'no harassment' clauses are therefore needed in management agreements with the hotel or hostel; in licenses granted to occupiers; and in any 'house rules'.

Investigation procedures should be similar to those used in mainstream tenancies. Residents should be informed how to make a complaint.

Not all residents may have been placed in the accommodation by the same local authority, so liaison may be required – LAs should inform one another of allegations and agree a joint course of action if staff/management are implicated.

Social landlords should cease to use or recommend any hotel or hostel where the management or staff have been involved in racial harassment, or have failed to take action to deal with it when reported.

London boroughs operate a joint management agreement with B&B hotels which contains the following terms:

The Hotel must ensure that its management practices comply with the Race Relations Act 1976 and the Sex Discrimination Act 1975, as amended. These Acts make it unlawful for a landlord or anyone managing the premises to discriminate on racial or sexual grounds in the treatment of anyone occupying the premises:

a) by refusing or deliberately omitting to give them access to normal benefits or facilities or in the way such access is provided;

b) by evicting them or subjecting them to any other harassment.

This covers such acts as providing inferior services to one particular group of residents because of their race or sex, imposing unnecessary rules on one particular group, using racially or sexually abusive language, and physically intimidating or assaulting residents because of their race or sex.

The Hotel should note that the employer is liable for any discrimination by any employee, whether or not it is done with the knowledge or approval of the employer.

The Hotel must particularly note the provisions of the following sections of the Race Relations Act 1976 – sections 1, 2, 20, 21, 30, 31, 32 and 33.

The Hotel's attention is drawn to the provisions of the Chronically Sick and Disabled Persons Act 1970.

9 The private sector

Purchasers of Right to Buy and shared ownership properties

Landlords can include a covenant in the lease (for flats) or a restricted covenant in the conveyance (for freehold properties). These can be enforced against all future owners of the property.

Where leaseholders are experiencing harassment from LA or HA tenants, many of the measures listed earlier will still be appropriate.

Owner occupiers and households in the private rented sector

Local authorities can provide or fund advice and assistance to address racial harassment in all tenures. The CRE *Code of Practice for non Rented Housing* (CRE 1992) suggests that LAs could provide an effective advisory/support service in conjunction with the strategies agreed for their own tenants. Liaison with the police and other agencies and information and publicity campaigns may also be appropriate. Local authorities may also wish to consider legal action under section 222 of the Local Government Act 1972 (for example, seeking injunctions where this is for the protection or promotion of the interests of their inhabitants).

Both local authorities and housing associations may wish to take racial harassment into account in assessing the priority of people applying for social housing.

> Leicester City Council awards additional points for council housing to victims of racial harassment living in the private sector.
>
> The Community Safety Unit in Rochdale provides advice and grant aid to improve home security.
>
> LB Hackney provides advice to private sector complainants and holds a case conference to determine the eligibility of those applying for rehousing via the council. Owner occupiers can apply to the Environmental Health Service for a means tested grant to enhance security.
>
> LB Barking and Dagenham recently obtained a possession order against one of its tenants who was harassing an owner occupier. The authority was prepared to offer temporary accommodation to the owner occupier for the period while the case was progressing, although in the event this was not needed.
>
> LB Hillingdon has approved a scheme under which the Housing Service will buy back homes sold under the Right to Buy in a number of circumstances, one of which includes the owner occupier suffering from racial harassment. In a recent case, temporary accommodation was arranged for the victim pending the buy-back, and they were subsequently rehoused by a local housing association.

10   Racial harassment and the law

This section provides a very brief outline of the law in England and Wales, and of proposed changes that may make it easier to obtain possession against perpetrators. Much more detailed guidance is provided in the references that follow. A working knowledge of legal remedies against perpetrators – and of their own legal obligations as service providers – is essential for housing staff who deal regularly with complaints of racial harassment, but does not of course remove the need to obtain qualified legal advice.

Legal remedies

There is no specific criminal offence of racial harassment, but the behaviour involved is frequently a breach of criminal law. Cases involving housing-related racial harassment are more commonly pursued in the civil courts, however, where the available remedies include injunctions and possession proceedings.

Criminal law covers public order offences (including offences relating to racial hatred) and breaches of property and planning law (including protection from eviction) as well as offences against people or property. A new offence of causing intentional harassment, alarm or distress was introduced in s.154 of the Criminal Justice and Public Order Act 1994, punishable by a prison term of up to six months and/or a fine. Local authorities can take part in criminal proceedings when this is for the protection or promotion of the interests of the inhabitants of their area (s.222 Local Government Act 1972) and are specifically authorised to prosecute under the Protection from Eviction Act 1977.

LAs also have the power to institute civil proceedings when they consider it expedient for the protection or promotion of the interests of the inhabitants of their area (s.222 Local Government Act 1972).

Injunctions can be used by both LAs and HAs to enforce the terms of the tenancy agreement, conveyance or lease; and to restrain a perpetrator (whether or not a tenant) from committing nuisance or trespass. They can also be obtained in the course of possession proceedings. There is more information and advice about injunctions (including a discussion of the pros and cons) in Duncan Forbes book (see below).

Repossession of secure and assured tenancies

In these types of tenancy, possession can be granted by the courts for:

1   breach of an express clause in a tenancy agreement;

2   causing nuisance or annoyance to neighbours;

3   waste to common parts (eg graffiti in communal areas).

All three grounds are discretionary – the courts are not obliged to grant possession, even when the facts are not in dispute. They will consider whether or not it is reasonable to make an order (taking into account, for example, the tenant's personal circumstances) and may decide to give them another chance by granting a suspended order. In relation to (2) above, under current law victims of racial harassment or other nuisance usually have to give evidence in court, and the statutory nuisance ground does not cover nuisance that is caused *by* visitors or *to* people who are not immediate neighbours. These limitations are addressed in the housing bill currently before Parliament (see below).

Repossession of assured shorthold tenancies

Although registered housing associations are normally required by the *Tenants' Guarantee* to grant assured tenancies in their general needs properties, the Housing Corporation has recently authorised a number of experimental schemes in which new tenants are initially granted assured shorthold tenancies (ASTs). At the end of the initial term, most ASTs will be converted into an ordinary assured tenancy. Where there has been anti social behaviour such as racial harassment, however, landlords will have the option of seeking possession. Provided the correct procedures are followed, the courts do not have discretion to refuse repossession of an AST and it is not necessary to provide any formal grounds. An accelerated court procedure is available and the victims of the anti social behaviour do not have to give evidence.

The granting of these 'introductory tenancies' makes it easier for housing associations to deal with people who perpetrate racial harassment early on in their tenure of an HA property. It is important, however, that associations do not allow themselves to be duped by malicious accusations of anti social behaviour – as might be made, for example, by someone who does not wish to have a black neighbour. HAs will therefore need to consider carefully the level and type of evidence required. At the time of writing, housing association introductory tenancies are still being evaluated and it is not known whether they will become more generally available. However, the Government is legislating to allow local authorities to operate similar introductory tenancies if they so choose (see below).

Other legal powers

Under section 137 of the Local Government Act 1972, local authorities have powers to fund advice and support services and monitoring groups concerned with racial harassment in all tenures.

LB Southwark has obtained numerous injunctions. Arrangements for victim and witness protection include mobile phones with pre-programmed emergency numbers, overnight stays, and professional security guards at the weekend.

Rochdale MBC has obtained 12 successful prosecutions for neighbourhood nuisance.

Hounslow LBC has funded private prosecutions by tenants.

London and Quadrant Housing Trust funded a successful defence against an injunction that was taken out against their tenant as part of the harassment.

Provisions of the Housing Bill 1996

The current Housing Bill contains a number of provisions that will, if enacted, be of direct relevance in tackling racial harassment. The comments below apply to the version of the Bill as amended in Standing Committee (April 1996).

Repossession of tenancies on grounds of nuisance – this will be extended to conduct which was, *or is likely to have been*, a nuisance or annoyance. The change of wording is intended to make it easier for the courts to accept evidence from professional witnesses such as housing officers or the police, thereby reducing the need for victims to testify when they may be at risk of retaliation. The amended ground will apply to nuisance from visitors as well as residents, and will protect visitors and anyone lawfully in the locality, rather than just neighbours or adjoining occupiers as at present. Identical nuisance grounds have been drafted for both secure and assured tenancies.

Possession procedures – these will be speeded up where nuisance is specified as one of the grounds. Under the Housing Bill it will be possible to speed up the repossession process by enabling a landlord to start possession proceedings against a tenant as soon as a notice for possession has been issued, rather than waiting 28 days (in the case of local authorities) or two weeks (for other social and private sector landlords) as at present. If the court agrees that it is just and equitable to do so, local authorities will be able to dispense with the issuing of a notice of intention to seek possession, bringing local authorities in line with other social and private landlords

Arrest for anti social behaviour – it will be possible for local authorities and registered social landlords to apply to the courts to have a power of arrest attached to injunctions against a breach of the tenancy. The breach must involve actual or threatened violence against an occupant or visitor or someone lawfully in the vicinity, and the court must be satisfied that there is a significant risk of harm if a power of arrest is not attached. As with the nuisance ground for possession, the tenant to whom the injunction applies need not necessarily be the perpetrator – this could be a fellow occupant or visitor that the tenant allows to act in this way. The power of arrest can only be exercised by the police.

This provision responds to the concern of many social landlords that injunctions without the power of arrest are of limited value. It will apply to introductory tenancies and to tenancies granted in pursuance of LA duties to the homeless, as well as to secure and assured tenancies. It will be possible to obtain these injunctions ex parte (ie without first notifying the person to whom it will apply) if the court is satisfied as to the urgency of the case or if it has reason to believe that the person is deliberately evading service of notice. The latter will then be given an early opportunity to make representations to the court.

LAs will, in addition, be able to seek to have the power of arrest attached to injunctions granted under section 222 of the Local Government Act (protection or promotion of the interests of inhabitants). This provision will apply in the same circumstances and to the same types of tenancy: the difference is that the injunction and power of arrest can be used to restrain someone who is not the tenant and not in breach of the tenancy agreement. Similar safeguards will apply.

Introductory tenancies – local authorities will be given the right to house new tenants for a 12 month trial period before the tenancy becomes secure. As with housing association ASTs, this will make it much easier to evict someone who is responsible for racial attacks and harassment early on in their tenancy.

- If a local authority wishes to implement an introductory tenancy scheme, it must apply to *all* new tenancies (other than transfers). LAs will not be allowed to choose to put some people 'on probation' whilst granting immediate secure tenancies to others.

- A court order will still be required to terminate an introductory tenancy. However, the court must grant an order if the LA has served a proper notice stating its intention to seek possession and giving its reasons. The tenant will be given seven days to request an internal review by the LA and must be notified of the result, and of the reasons if the decision to seek possession is upheld.

- The DoE will be issuing guidance to local authorities on the practical operation of introductory tenancies. LAs will be encouraged to adopt fair and rigorous procedures that will command the confidence of tenants and ensure that no one's home is put at risk because of malicious or bogus complaints.

Legal duties

Sections 20-21 of the Race Relations Act 1976 outlaw discrimination in the provision of goods and services, including the disposal or management of premises. Failure to deal effectively with racial harassment may in some circumstances contravene these sections. Sections 30-32 outlaw instructions to discriminate and pressure to discriminate, and make employers responsible for the actions of their staff.

Under s.71 of the Act, local authorities, the Housing Corporation and Housing Action Trusts have a duty to eliminate unlawful discrimination and to promote equality of opportunity and good race relations.

The CRE's *Code of Practice in Rented Housing* (1991) applies to all housing organisations in England, Scotland and Wales. The code does not impose any legal obligations itself, but its provisions may be taken into account in any proceedings under the Race Relations Act. It contains a section on racial harassment with recommendations on victim support, action against perpetrators, and working with staff, tenants and other agencies.

Compliance with the CRE Code of Practice is one of the criteria for registration of a housing association – this requirement is reiterated in the *Tenants' Guarantee*, in which the Housing Corporation states that registered associations are expected explicitly to endorse the CRE code.

The Housing Bill currently before Parliament includes provisions to enable non-profit-making landlords to register with, and compete for grants from, the Housing Corporation. Such landlords might include local housing companies set up to receive transfers of local authority stock. All social landlords registered in this way will have the same responsibilities in respect of the Tenants' Guarantee and the CRE Code of Practice as existing associations.

The current legislation on homelessness provides that a person shall not be treated as having accommodation available for occupation unless it is accommodation which it would be reasonable for him/her to continue to occupy. The Homelessness Code of Guidance for Local Authorities (revised third edition, 1994) lists various factors local authorities should take into account before reaching a decision on this matter, including violence or threats of violence from outside the home:

> *The authority will need to consider the seriousness of the violence, or threats of violence, the frequency of occurrence and the likelihood of reoccurrence. Violence or threats of violence could include racial harassment or attacks; violence against a person; sexual abuse or harassment and harassment on the grounds of religious creed.*

10a Sources of further advice on the law

Action on Racial Harassment: Legal Remedies and Local Authorities by Duncan Forbes (1988) gives a comprehensive account of the powers and responsibilities of local authorities and the civil and criminal sanctions that can be used to protect tenants. It also contains practical advice on collecting evidence and interviewing. Much of the material covered is equally relevant to housing associations. A revised edition is due to be published in 1996 – further details from the Legal Action Group, 242 Pentonville Road, London N1 9UN.

Nuisance and Harassment: Law and Practice in the Management of Social Housing by Susan Belgrave, volume 3 of Arden's Housing Library, Lemos Associates (now Lemos and Crane), 1995.

Home Office Circular 30/1995, **Racial attacks and harassment,** outlines the legal powers available to combat racially-motivated crime, including the new offence of intentional harassment and new powers of arrest.

The new offence of intentional harassment and its applicability to racial harassment in a housing context is reviewed by two housing barristers in **Leading Edge, Issue 2** – an occasional briefing available from Lemos and Crane.

Getting the Best Out of the Court System: Guidance for Local Authorities, DoE, Lord Chancellor's Department and Welsh Office, 1996. Covers court procedures – highlighting ways in which it is possible to get possession cases heard quickly in cases of anti-social behaviour – and ways of protecting and reassuring witnesses.

Advice on possession procedures is also given in section 9 of the **Housing Management Standards Manual,** Chartered Institute of Housing (the manual is regularly updated).

11 Competitive tendering of housing management

Local authorities are required to seek competitive tenders for 95 per cent of housing management services falling within certain 'defined activities'. They have discretion over the remaining 5 per cent, and can also decide whether to retain or seek tenders for services which are not defined activities.

Informing tenants of the terms of their tenancies and taking steps to enforce these terms are defined activities, as is taking steps to resolve disputes between neighbours. On the other hand, investigating harassment, allocating properties, and community development work are not defined activities for the purposes of housing management CCT.

Local authorities will need to look carefully at the packaging of housing management functions in relation to racial harassment procedures, in order to achieve a smooth relationship between contracted-out services and those retained within the council (some of which may be in departments other than housing).

When preparing tender and contract documentation, LAs should have regard to CCT legislation and guidance, together with the EC procurement rules as appropriate. Department of the Environment Circular 5/96 'Guidance on the Conduct of Compulsory Competitive Tendering' provides statutory guidance on the conduct of CCT and indicates that LAs are encouraged to adopt output based (specified in terms of the results to be achieved) rather than input (specified in terns of working) specifications. This allows tenderers to develop alternative ways of delivering the service and to innovate. However, it is accepted that input and process measures may be appropriate where outputs are difficult to frame.

Output based specifications may require tenderers to submit method statements, but these should be used sparingly and limited to those areas where there is a critical interface either with customers or clients. Tenderers should only be asked to provide method statements where it is necessary for LAs to form a view on their proposals for delivering the outputs sought and their competence and experience to carry out the work.

In selecting tenderers, LAs may ask six approved questions about a firm's race relations policy, reflecting their statutory duty under the Race Relations Act 1976. Guidance on race relations during the contractual process is set out in DoE Circular 8/88.

Finally

The Racial Attacks Group will be following up its previous reports in 1989 and 1991 (see references) with a new report in 1996. It will also be publishing a guide to undertaking local surveys of racial harassment. This will explain how to assess the extent of the problem and the extent of under-reporting, and suggest how agencies can evaluate the effectiveness of their response.

The Government's Inner Cities Religious Council is producing a guide on religious discrimination, to be published in 1996. The areas covered will include housing, education, social services, health and benefits.

Lemos and Crane will be publishing a book on supporting those experiencing racial harassment in 1996.

The London Research Centre is compiling a directory of initiatives against racial harassment, on behalf of Lemos and Crane. The directory will detail the work of around 180 organisations in England, Scotland and Wales, including local authorities, housing associations, racial equality councils, voluntary organisations, community groups, and legal and advice centres. Further information from Lemos and Crane, 20 Pond Square, London N6 6BA 0181 348 8263.

Part 2   Research report

12   Summary and conclusions

Aims

12.1 The research described in this report had two purposes:

    (i)   to examine the extent to which previous good practice guidelines have been taken up by social landlords;

    (ii)   to provide a housing perspective on multi-agency work, as part of a wider information-gathering exercise for the inter-departmental Racial Attacks Group (a report was subsequently submitted to the RAG in early 1995).

Method

12.2 The Department of the Environment had carried out a postal survey of English local authorities in 1991, and now wished to update this information and extend it to housing associations. A questionnaire was mailed in October 1994 to 335 local authorities and 263 of the larger housing associations (those with 250 or more general needs properties). As with the 1991 survey, many landlords had insufficient experience of dealing with racial harassment to complete a questionnaire. They were invited instead to indicate whether they had policies and procedures in place should the need arise.

Response

12.3 90 per cent of the landlords responded, with 34 per cent completing the full questionnaire and 56 per cent opting out on grounds of lack of experience or lack of policy development. The overall response from housing associations and local authorities was similar, but the former were more likely to complete the full questionnaire.

Policies on racial harassment

12.4 The overall response indicates that less than half of English local authority housing departments have written policies and procedures on racial harassment, compared with nine out of ten of the larger housing associations. However, it can be estimated from this response that more than four out of five black and ethnic minority council tenants in England are renting from a landlord that does have a policy.

Changes in local authorities since 1991

12.5 Certain key elements of good practice have spread since the previous survey, with a growing proportion of local authorities in multi racial areas now implementing various aspects of prevention, victim support and action against perpetrators. For example, the large majority of respondents to the full questionnaire are now publicising their policies, inserting clauses on racial harassment into tenancy agreements, and keeping ethnic records on applicants for housing. Closer inspection of the 1991 and 1994 responses suggests that progress can be erratic, however.

12.6 There has been less policy development in respect of people who are not in secure or assured tenancies: owner occupiers, private renters, Right to Buy leaseholders, shared owners, and people in the various forms of temporary accommodation used by housing associations and local authorities.

Local authorities compared with housing associations

12.7 Housing associations have less experience of dealing with racial harassment than local authorities and have taken correspondingly less action against perpetrators. On the other hand, associations have been somewhat more active in trying to prevent harassment from occurring in the first place.

12.8 Few housing associations currently inform anyone outside of their immediate organisation about the level of racial harassment being reported to them, and they are equally unlikely to receive such information from elsewhere. They are much less likely than local authority housing departments to be involved in multi-agency groups, or even to know of their existence.

Perpetrators

12.9 In dealing with perpetrators, very few cases are pursued all the way to prosecution or eviction. This reflects both the difficulty of getting through the process (collecting evidence, liaison with legal staff, persuading people to act as witnesses) *and* the fact that some perpetrators stop their behaviour in response to a visit, warning letter or injunction.

Tenants' associations and community groups

12.10 Comparatively little work is being done with tenants' and residents' associations. For example, fewer than one in five of the landlords that completed the questionnaire inform TAs when an incident has taken place on the estate, and less than one in ten give tenant representatives any statistics on the level of harassment. Fewer than one in ten multi-agency groups contains a tenant representative.

12.11 In some areas there is also a certain ambivalence about community groups: contacts are poorly developed; a few local authorities are frustrated at their inability to get groups involved in the multi-agency process; and there is concern that lack of resources is preventing the participation of groups that might otherwise be willing.

Multi-agency groups

12.12 Most participants in multi-agency groups thought that this method of working had distinct advantages. But there are problems, particularly when not all agencies show the same level of commitment. The continuing inability of some groups to agree a basic issue such the working definition of racial harassment may be a symptom of this.

Suggestions for improving practice

The need for a policy

12.13 Recognising the existence of racial harassment and having policies and procedures in place to deal with it is an important starting point. The vulnerability of someone who is being racially harassed is made worse if housing staff have not been trained and equipped to recognise and deal with the situation. Nearly all large housing associations have policies and procedures in place should the need arise. It would be advisable for local authorities to do likewise. Both the DoE guidance (sent to local authorities in 1989 but now out of print) and the more recent guide published by Lemos Associates (1994) can be used by staff who have not yet had experience of dealing with racial harassment. Good practice recommendations from these and other publications are summarised in Part 1.

Non traditional tenures

12.14 In the same spirit of preparedness, both local authorities and housing associations should ensure that their policies and procedures are applicable to all the tenure categories, temporary and permanent, in which they are involved. The Chartered Institute of Housing recommends, for example, that social landlords make it a condition of contracts with managing agents and with suppliers of temporary accommodation that they comply with the landlord's policies on harassment and provide monitoring reports of any such incidents occurring in accommodation they manage on the landlord's behalf. The CIH also recommends that the idea of an anti- racial harassment clause in tenancy agreements can be extended to licence agreements and covenants (the latter on the sale of the landlord's dwellings).

Co-operation between social landlords

12.15 There was evidence from the survey that local authorities and housing associations were co-operating in a variety of ways, often outside of formal multi-agency arrangements. At present this is largely confined to rehousing issues, but local authorities have access to other resources that may be of assistance, particularly to smaller associations. These include, for example, their in-house legal staff (some of whom have accumulated expertise in racial harassment casework), press and information officers, youth and community workers, researchers, and the resources and expertise of social services and education departments.

Multi-agency groups

12.16 The use of a common incident form has improved monitoring in some areas. More could be done to involve housing associations by trying to ensure that the associations working in each area have a collective representative on the multi-agency group and that information flows in both directions. Tenants, legal staff and community groups are not well represented on multi-agency groups at present, although there are good reasons for involving all three.

Information exchange

12.17 As far as the collection and exchange of information is concerned, it may be helpful for both internal and inter-agency working parties to make a clearer separation between the information needed for investigation purposes; for monitoring of incidents and policy development; and for monitoring and evaluation of the response to racial harassment. These functions may also require input from different types of staff.

Monitoring performance

12.18 There is a continuing need for performance measures to ensure that visits, interviews, investigations, repairs, security measures, graffiti removal and transfers are all completed to a deadline, but it is also important to obtain direct feedback from those experiencing harassment. Some landlords in the survey were maintaining regular contact with victims to make sure there was no recurrence of the harassment and to keep them informed of the progress of investigations, but few appeared to obtain the victim's own assessment of their performance and pass this on to management committees or multi-agency groups.

Tenants' and residents' associations

12.19 Tenants' and residents' associations have the potential to be both part of the problem and part of the solution to racial harassment. They can help promote awareness amongst tenants about equal opportunities and harassment issues and can provide feedback to landlords on local problems. TAs also play a vital role in consultations about the management and rehabilitation of eststes and it is therefore important that they reflect the needs and concerns of all ethnic groups. The authors of a recent guide (TPAS, 1995) carried out preparatory research which included a questionnaire survey of 162 local authorities and 133 housing associations. They conclude: 'Our research has identified few examples of good practice but plenty of good intentions'.

12.20 Formally established tenants' associations and tenant management organisations should be required to incorporate policies on equal opportunities, harassment and discrimination into their constitutions. The Chartered Institute of Housing recommends in its Housing Management Standards Manual that this be made a condition of recognition, funding, and the use of the landlord's premises. Landlords should work closely with tenant groups to encourage and monitor the implementation of these policies, and involve them in training and multi agency arrangements. There is guidance for social landlords on working with TAs in several recent publications (TPAS 1995, CATCH 1994, CRE 1993b).

Legal advice

12.21 Social landlords experiencing a high incidence of racial attacks and harassment may wish to consider the use of one or more 'dedicated' legal officers who work full time on racial harassment cases. Such staff would also be able to make an invaluable contribution to multi-agency groups – the latter appear to have little direct access to legal advice at present. Landlords experiencing fewer incidents could seek out a firm of solicitors with experience in this area.

Staff training

12.22 There was some evidence from the survey that well conducted interviews with perpetrators can be effective. Recent guidelines (Lemos Associates, 1993) are particularly useful in this respect. Housing staff also require training in other tasks such as interviewing witnesses and collecting evidence.

13   Introduction and background to the study

13.1 The House of Commons Home Affairs Committee, reporting on racial attacks and harassment in 1986, stated that the incidence of such attacks is 'the most shameful and dispiriting aspect of race relations in Britain'. The Committee also noted: 'Of the local authority departments with responsibility in respect of racial incidents, housing departments are the most closely involved'.

13.2 In a subsequent report in 1989 the Home Affairs Committee noted that, according to a Home Office analysis of police statistics, 26 per cent of racially motivated incidents took place on local authority housing estates.

13.3 Racial violence and harassment in or near the home is especially threatening. Perpetrators know where the victim can be found and may themselves live nearby, so the potential for repetition and escalation is high. A recent study of repeat racial victimisation on a housing estate in East London found that most perpetrators were either immediate neighbours or lived very close to their victims (Home Office, 1995). The response of local authorities and housing associations, in their role as landlords to either or both parties, is of critical importance. The first comprehensive guide for local housing authorities on ways of combating racial violence was published by the Commission for Racial Equality in 1981. It urged careful monitoring of all incidents and the development of a coherent inter agency strategy, which should be monitored to ensure its effectiveness.

13.4 Since that time, a great deal more good practice advice has been published. In England, local authorities have received guidance from the Department of the Environment (1989) and from their own local authority associations (1987). Housing associations have been advised by the National Federation of Housing Associations (1982, 1983 and 1989) and registered associations are required by the Housing Corporation to comply with the Commission for Racial Equality's Code of Practice in the field of rented housing (1991) and the NFHA's recommendations. The CRE itself, the Chartered Institute of Housing, and numerous other organisations, large and small, have all made further contributions (eg CRE 1987 and CIH 1995).

13.5 The CRE's Code of Practice on rented housing includes a number of recommendations in relation to victim support, action against perpetrators and working with staff, tenants and local agencies. The sister *Code of Practice for non-Rented (Owner-Occupied) Housing* urges local authorities to provide an effective advisory/support service to owner occupiers. Both codes have been endorsed by Parliament and while neither imposes legal obligations, failure to observe the recommendations may be taken into account in any proceedings under the Race Relations Act.

13.6 In its 1986 report, the Home Affairs Committee emphasised the importance of a multi-agency approach to racial incidents. Police forces and local authorities whose areas contained an 'appreciable' ethnic minority population were urged to give serious consideration to the establishment of such an approach. This recommendation was strongly endorsed by the Government in its response (1986). To assist this process, the Home Office set up a Racial Attacks Group whose membership was drawn from government departments and other agencies, including the police and the Commission for Racial Equality. The RAG issued guidance for statutory agencies in 1989 and a second report in 1991.

13.7 The DoE's good practice guide was sent to English housing authorities in 1989. The Department carried out a postal survey in 1991 with the twin aims of assessing the extent to which its own recommendations had been taken up, and evaluating the response to the RAG report, with its recommendations for multi-agency working. The results of this research were published in 1994.

13.8 The Racial Attacks Group's second report in 1991 reviewed progress in the light of the feedback provided by the DoE and other government departments and provided further examples of good practice. The second report concluded that no further policy guidance was necessary: it was a question of implementing what had already been recommended. The Group expressed concern that their recommendations were not always getting through to the people who needed to implement them.

13.9 The present research was a follow up to the DoE's 1991 survey. It had the same aims: to examine the extent to which good practice guidelines had been taken up by landlords and to provide a housing perspective on multi-agency working for the Racial Attacks Group, which had reconvened in 1994. Some of the questions asked in 1991 were repeated, to allow for direct comparisons, and the survey was extended to cover housing associations.

13.10 When the CRE first published guidelines in 1981, local authorities were still the main providers of new social rented housing (this role has now been taken over by housing associations) and it was relatively rare for LAs to be providing any type of accommodation other than permanent tenancies in council-owned dwellings. Since that time, an increase in the number of homeless acceptances has led to an expansion in the various forms of temporary accommodation; implementation of the Right to Buy has created a new generation of freeholders and leaseholders in the midst of council estates; and social landlords have been promoting shared ownership schemes for people who cannot afford the full cost of mortgage repayments.

13.11 All these developments have changed the context in which racial harassment can occur. Even when victims and perpetrators live next door to one another, they may no longer share the same landlord. Many housing association tenants, and homeless households placed in properties leased from private sector landlords, do not live on estates at all, but in street properties surrounded by owner occupiers or private tenants. The legal sanctions that can be used against perpetrators may vary, depending on whether he or she is a secure tenant, assured tenant, leaseholder or licensee. It was therefore a further aim of the survey to make a brief assessment of the extent to which social landlords seemed to be prepared for these situations.

Research method   13.12 Questionnaires were sent to 598 social landlords (335 English local authorities and 263 of the larger housing associations) in October 1994. It was recognised at the outset that there would be many local authorities and associations with insufficient experience of dealing with racial harassment to make it feasible for them to complete the whole questionnaire. These landlords were asked instead to indicate whether they were not completing the full questionnaire because they had no *experience* of racial harassment; no *policies or procedures* for dealing with it; or both. This is a similar procedure to that used by the DoE in its 1991 survey of local authorities.

13.13 Further details of the fieldwork are given in Annex 1 and the questionnaire is reproduced at Annex 2.

Response   13.14 Thirty four per cent of landlords completed the full questionnaire and 56 per cent returned the short questionnaire, giving an overall response of 90 per cent. Because of late returns, most of the quantitative analysis in this report is based on the 87 per cent of landlords (295 local authorities and 222 housing associations) who replied before the deadline. Annex 1 gives full details of the response, including a breakdown of the local authority response for each DoE region.

13.15 The number of respondents choosing to complete each type of questionnaire is shown in Table 1.

Table 1 Type of landlord and choice of questionnaire				
	Short	Full	Total	% opting for full questionnaire
London Boroughs	4	25	29	86
Metropolitan authorities outside London	9	24	33	73
District councils	192	54	246	22
All local authorities	205	103	308	33
Housing associations	128	100	228	44
All landlords	333	203	536	38

Base: all respondents including late returns.

13.16 The proportion of local authorities choosing the full questionnaire in 1994 (33 per cent) was very similar to that in the 1991 survey (32 per cent). At 44 per cent, the proportion of housing associations completing the full questionnaire was somewhat higher than local authorities. This is probably a reflection of the emphasis placed by the Housing Corporation and the NFHA on the need for policies and procedures in this area, rather than an indication that associations have more experience of racial harassment (see Chapter 2).

13.17 The choice of questionnaire made by local authorities in each region is shown in Table 2.

Table 2 Region and choice of questionnaire (local authorities)				
	Short	Full	Total	% opting for full questionnaire
London	4	25	29	86
North	16	5	21	24
Yorkshire and Humberside	14	9	23	39
East Midlands	29	10	39	26
Eastern	28	10	38	26
South East	39	13	52	25
South West	31	6	37	16
West Midlands	20	9	29	31
North West	24	16	40	40

Base: all respondents including late returns.

13.18 After London, the North West and Yorkshire and Humberside produced the highest proportions of fully completed questionnaires, and the South West the lowest.

13.19 Some housing associations operate across a very wide geographical area and a few of these chose to complete more than one questionnaire. This process produced a total of seven extra respondents, each of whom were treated in the analysis as if they were a separate association.

14 Racial incidents recorded by social landlords

14.1 It is very difficult to get reliable statistics about the level of racially motivated attacks and harassment. Many cases go unreported, particularly in areas where there is a low level of trust between statutory agencies and local ethnic minority communities. In addition, some incidents are reported to but not recorded by the statutory agencies. For example, although police statistics on racial incidents are supposed to include complaints about behaviour that is not technically criminal, such incidents may not always be recorded in practice. And in spite of victim-centred definitions, it is possible that landlords do not always record complaints which they do not consider to be racially motivated.

Sources of information

Police statistics

14.2 11,878 racial incidents were recorded by the police in England and Wales in 1994/5[2], of which 46 per cent were recorded in the Metropolitan area. When examining police statistics, it is almost impossible to say whether changes over time (or variations between one part of the country and another) reflect the actual pattern of incidents; changes in the level of reporting; or differences in recording practice. Exactly the same comments can be made about the housing-related incidents recorded by local authorities and housing associations.

British Crime Survey

14.3 Because of the shortcomings of police and other statistics, greater reliance is often placed on survey methods for measuring the level of racial harassment. The British Crime Survey, in particular, has the advantage of national coverage and a time series covering a number of years. In the 1988, 1992 and 1994 surveys there was a booster sample of Afro-Caribbean and Asian households.

14.4 It was estimated from the 1992 survey that there were 130,000 offences in England and Wales in 1991 which were either racially motivated, or where some element of racial abuse was present (Home Office, 1994). Around a quarter of these incidents involved an assault, and about 60 per cent involved threats or vandalism.

14.5 These figures largely reflect incidents that were judged to be criminal offences and not the 'low level' harassment to which ethnic minority groups are also subject. Since the question about motivation was only asked of the Asian and Afro-Caribbean sample, they also exclude harassment of other ethnic groups such as Irish people.

---

[2] Hansard, 29 March 1996.

Local surveys

14.6 Whilst these are a valuable source of information, they are difficult to compare because of variations in definition, sampling techniques and periods of reference. Most such surveys have examined racial harassment generally, rather than housing-related incidents. A number of respondents to the questionnaire had been involved in local surveys and there is more information on the uses to which the data were put in Chapter 19 of this report.

Records held by social landlords

14.7 The incidents recorded by social landlords differ from the above sources of information in two important ways:

- they are generally housing-related, and do not include incidents at work, school or elsewhere;

- they include all 'levels' of incident from name-calling to serious crimes – although the least serious are probably the least likely to be reported.

14.8 In relation to the second point, it is important to stress that the extent to which people report incidents is affected by their confidence in the willingness or ability of the authorities to do anything. Some cases only come to light when they result in damage to property needing repair, or when the victims are driven to seek a transfer. Fear of reprisals, language difficulties, and a sense of shame at being repeatedly victimised and having to ask for assistance have also been identified as barriers to reporting (Home Office, 1995).

Racial harassment as a cause of housing transfers

14.9 Although there is no national data on the subject, recent research for the DoE (1994b) has suggested that racial harassment is a growing component of management transfers in metropolitan areas.

14.10 Very few attempts have been made to collate data on the extent to which racial attacks and harassment generate transfer requests, or to establish whether landlords' response to such requests is as victim-led as policies sometimes imply. Competing pressures on relets or the desire not to 'hand perpetrators a victory' are both factors that may cause transfer requests to be delayed, perhaps indefinitely. Analysis of data collected from 13 London boroughs by the London Research Centre (1992) suggests that in a year when the housing departments concerned recorded over 1,000 incidents, there were some 450 transfer requests and 179 actual moves.

Racial harassment in the housing stock of respondents who did not complete the full questionnaire

14.11 As stated in Chapter 13, social landlords with little or no experience of dealing with racial harassment were given the opportunity to opt out of the full questionnaire. Housing associations were rather more likely to complete the full questionnaire (44 per cent) than local authorities (33 per cent). This does not mean that they have more experience of dealing with racial harassment than local authorities: in fact it can be seen from Tables 4 and 6 later that associations are generally dealing with fewer cases. Most of the associations in the survey have far fewer properties than the local authorities in whose areas they operate, so other things (such as the percentage of ethnic minority tenants) being equal they ought to have had less experience of racial harassment. On the other hand, some associations operate over wider geographical areas than local authorities and may therefore be more likely to encounter harassment somewhere in their stock.

14.12 Landlords opting out of the full questionnaire were asked to say whether this was because they had little or no experience of racial harassment in their housing stock; no policies or procedures for responding to racial harassment; or both (see Annex 2).

14.13 The reason for separating policy and procedure from experience in this way was that all registered housing associations are required to have procedures in place by the Housing Corporation, and it was anticipated that many might have written policies that had not yet been put to the test. It was felt that local authorities, on the other hand, would be less likely to have policies and procedures in place unless racial harassment was already perceived to be a problem locally. The results of the survey largely confirmed this view.

Table 3 Reason for not completing the full questionnaire

	LAs	%	HAs	%	All landlords	%
Little or no experience of RH and no policies/procedures for dealing with it	142	70	16	13	158	48
Policies but little or no experience	54	27	106	85	160	49
Experienced RH but no policies	5	2	2	2	7	2
Other reason	1	–	1	1	2	1
Total (100%)	202		125		327	

Base: respondents to short questionnaire, excluding late returns.

14.14 Ninety seven per cent of the landlords opting out of the full questionnaire gave lack of experience of racial harassment as the reason. Overall, these were almost equally divided between those that had policies and procedures should the need arise, and those that did not. However, there was a marked difference – as expected – between local authorities and housing associations. A large majority of the associations had policies and procedures in place, but this was true of only a small minority of the local authorities. Seven landlords admitted that racial harassment was a problem locally but they had not done anything about it.

14.15 A check on the local authorities completing the short questionnaire revealed that 80 per cent had fewer than 50 ethnic minority tenants at the time of the 1991 Census[3] so in many cases the claim of very few or no incidents of racial harassment locally may be justified. The major exception to this was a London borough with over 3,000 ethnic minority tenants, which returned the short questionnaire but indicated that policy development was taking place. The remaining respondents to

---

[3] The ethnic groups covered in the 1991 Census did not include Irish people.

the short questionnaire accounted, between them, for less than 5 per cent of the ethnic minority tenant population. This is not to say that the incidence of racial harassment in these areas (ie the percentage of people from minority groups who have been attacked, as opposed to the actual number of attacks) may not be quite high. Isolated people from minority groups in a predominantly white area may be more at risk than those on estates where black people are more numerous.

14.16 Unfortunately it is not possible to carry out a similar analysis on individual housing associations using Census data. However, the fact that a higher proportion of housing associations than local authorities opted for the full questionnaire suggests that a high proportion of those to whom racial harassment has been reported are represented in the findings described below.

Racial harassment in the housing stock of respondents to the full questionnaire

14.17 Table 4 gives some indication of the number of incidents reported to local authorities in the year before the survey (respondents could choose whether to give calendar year figures for 1993 or financial year figures for 1993/94). Respondents were not asked to provide information on incidents reported by owner occupiers and private rented tenants – this question would not have been applicable to housing associations and it seemed likely that few local authorities would have the information (as will be seen in Chapter 15, only about one in five local authority respondents had a policy on racial harassment in the private sector). They were, however, asked about incidents involving Right to Buy leaseholders or shared owners, and about incidents in various forms of temporary accommodation, including properties leased from the private sector (PSL).

Table 4 — Number of local authorities receiving reports of racial incidents from people in each tenure category in the year before the survey

Number of incidents	Number of local authorities to whom incidents reported:				
	Secure tenants	Hostels, B&B etc	PSL etc	RTB	Shared owners
None	9	19	16	19	19
1-9	32	13	7	9	0
10-19	14	1	1	1	0
20-49	15	0	1	0	0
50-99	7	0	1	0	0
100-199	7	0	0	0	0
200-299	1	0	0	0	0
300 or more	4	0	0	0	0
Records not kept	9	12	8	10	8
Tenure does not apply	0	5	15	3	12
No response	5	53	54	61	64
Total local authorities	103	103	103	103	103

Base: local authority respondents to the full questionnaire.
Note: table includes late returns because these included several London boroughs with a relatively large number of incidents.

14.18 Twenty per cent of the local authorities and 14 per cent of the housing associations stated that their figures related to the number of *households* reporting racial incidents rather then the number of *incidents* reported. Given that some households are subject to repeated attacks, the figures in the table underestimate the true level of reporting to the landlords in the survey. Landlords with higher levels of harassment in their stock are more likely to keep their records on a casework basis, so the underestimate may not be insignificant.

14.19 A significant feature of Table 4 is the large number of LAs that only provided information on secure tenancies. In order to minimise the time required to complete the questionnaire, respondents were asked to tick boxes alongside the categories shown rather than supply an exact number of incidents. Nevertheless, most respondents failed either to make an estimate or to indicate that records were not kept or that the tenure category was not applicable to their authority. The number that did provide information tallied reasonably well with the number that stated they had written policies and procedures covering the tenure category (see Chapter 15).

14.20 All five of the local authorities with 200 or more incidents in secure tenancies were London boroughs, as were four of the seven authorities with between 100 and 199 incidents.

14.21 It is difficult to comment on the frequency of harassment in temporary accommodation, Right to Buy or shared ownership properties without any information on the total stock of such units to which the figures relate. The much higher number of cases in secure tenancies may simply reflect the preponderance of the latter. Nearly all the incidents in the other tenure categories were recorded by those local authorities that had ten or more incidents in their permanent housing stock.

14.22 In 1991, 31 per cent of respondents to the full questionnaire failed to provide any data on the number of incidents reported in the year before the survey, so for secure tenancies at least Table 4 does suggest a significant improvement in recording practice.

14.23 Table 5 compares the percentage of local authorities in each incident category in the 1991 and 1994 surveys, based on those authorities that provided data.

14.24 The 1991 survey also asked for information about 1987/88 and 1988/89. In trying to compare these three years with the more recent data it would be very difficult to disentangle changes in reporting and recording practice from trends in the underlying level of racial attacks and harassment. An additional factor is that the practice of recording incidents of racial harassment is likely to have begun first in LAs where racial harassment is more common. The higher proportion of LAs in 1994 with few or no incidents in the previous year may simply reflect the spread of record-keeping to less affected areas.

Table 5 Local authorities receiving reports of incidents in 1989/90 and 1993

No. incidents reported by secure tenants	Percentage of LAs in each category in:	
	1989/90	1993 or 1993/94
None	3	10
1-9	28	36
10-19	24	16
20-49	21	17
50-99	9	8
100 or more	16	13

Base: 58 LAs in 1989/90 and 89 in 1993 or 1993/94.

14.25 Around 60-70 per cent of the incidents recorded by LAs were in London – this is comparable with the proportion of all ethnic minority council tenants who live in the capital (66 per cent at the 1991 Census).

14.26 The 1991 questionnaire was not sent to housing associations. Results from the 1994 survey are shown in Table 6. A few of the larger associations with regional structures completed more than one questionnaire, so the number of forms available for analysis was 107 rather than 100.

Table 6 Number of housing associations receiving reports of racial incidents from people in each tenure category in the year before the survey

Number of incidents	Number of housing associations to whom incidents reported				
	Secure or assured tenants	Hostels, short life etc	PSL etc	RTB	Shared owners
None	13	35	29	32	34
1-9	75	9	4	2	2
10-19	12	0	0	0	0
20-49	4	1	0	0	0
50-99	0	0	0	0	0
100-199	0	0	0	0	0
200-299	0	0	0	0	0
300 or more	0	0	0	0	0
Records not kept	3	4	4	4	4
Tenure does not apply	0	14	24	22	21
No response	0	44	46	47	46
Total associations	107	107	107	107	107

Base: HA respondents to the full questionnaire
Table includes late returns

14.27 Only three associations did not keep records of racial harassment reported by secure or assured tenants. 70 per cent of HA respondents were dealing with between 1 and 9 reports a year in such tenancies: fewer cases on average than local authorities, reflecting the smaller housing stocks of many associations.

14.28 Record-keeping by associations on incidents in other forms of tenure appeared to be less good, although it is possible that some of the non response was due to associations who failed to indicate that the tenure category did not apply to them. The number of associations able to provide information on each of the other tenure categories tied in reasonably well with the number that said they had policies for that category (see chapter 15). For example, 46 associations claimed that they had policies and procedures covering harassment in hostel or short life accommodation, and 45 were able to provide data on incidents.

14.29 Fifty seven landlords (42 local authorities and 15 housing associations) replied before the survey deadline to the effect that they had recorded ten or more incidents in their own housing stock in the previous year. This group will be referred to again throughout the report.

15 Policies on racial harassment

15.1 In 1991, nearly three quarters of the 85 local authorities that completed the full questionnaire said they had a policy statement and written procedure for dealing with racial violence and harassment. The number with policy statements or procedures amongst the 197 that completed the short questionnaire in 1991 is not known.

15.2 In 1994, over 90 per cent of LA respondents to the full questionnaire and 97 per cent of HA respondents said they had written policies and procedures. Combining their responses with those of associations and authorities replying to the short questionnaire, it seems that around 45 per cent of English local housing authorities have policies and procedures in respect of racial harassment, compared with around 90 per cent of the larger housing associations (these percentages may be somewhat lower if the 10 per cent of landlords who did not respond to the survey could be taken into account, although it is known that some of these also have policies). Although associations have clearly responded to the Corporation's and the NFHA's initiatives on the issue, there were still 19 HA respondents who admitted to having no policies and procedures, including two that said they had actually experienced racial harassment in their housing stock.

15.3 The local authorities with a written policy and procedure on racial harassment accounted for about 84 per cent of ethnic minority council tenants in England at the time of the 1991 Census. The equivalent figure for tenants of the larger housing associations could well be higher. Whilst such policies are no guarantee of an adequate response, they do at least provide a benchmark that can be used by people experiencing harassment and by their advocates.

Tenure categories covered by policies and procedures on racial harassment

15.4 The 1991 questionnaire did not specifically ask about racial harassment affecting people who were not secure tenants of the local authority but who might nevertheless look to the council for assistance in dealing with racial harassment related to their housing. This includes people in the categories described below.

Those placed by local authorities in various forms of temporary accommodation. This includes hostels, short life properties, bed and breakfast accommodation, and properties owned by private sector landlords. Such accommodation is used by some local authorities to house statutorily homeless households whilst their cases are being assessed or whilst waiting for a suitable vacancy in permanent council or housing association housing. Little is known about the incidence of racial harassment in hostels and bed and breakfast accommodation, but the communal environment and the stresses associated with homelessness hardly seem conducive to a lower incidence of harassment than that found elsewhere. Housing associations also manage hostels and short life properties, often using them to house single homeless people.

The use of properties owned by private sector landlords has increased in recent years, as local authorities have sought to avoid the expense and poor conditions in bed and breakfast hotels. Private rented properties are also being used by a few authorities as a way of permanently discharging their duties to the homeless, and this practice may spread in future. Again, little is known about the incidence of racial harassment in these properties. The accommodation is often of good quality and self-contained, but a black family placed in a street of white owner occupiers may not always get a warm welcome. Housing associations are often involved in managing or leasing the private rented properties that are used by local authorities for temporary accommodation.

People who have exercised the Right to Buy but continue to live on a local authority estate (for flat-owners, the local authority remains as their freeholder). Such people might be harassed by tenants or other leaseholders on the estate, or they may themselves be the perpetrators of harassment. The situation can apply, although less frequently, to housing associations since some HA tenants do have the Right to Buy (if the Housing Bill currently before Parliament is enacted, tenants of future HA schemes will be able to acquire their homes with a purchase grant).

People who are purchasing their homes on a shared ownership basis. Some housing associations, in particular, have specialised in providing this form of accommodation.

Other residents in the area (ie owner occupiers and private sector tenants who do not have any connection with a council housing department or housing association). Local authorities have legal powers that may be applicable in these circumstances, and some victims may approach them for advice. Local authorities in the survey were therefore asked whether their policies extended to the private sector generally.

15.5 Figure 1 shows the proportions of housing associations and local authorities completing the full questionnaire who said they had written policies and procedures when dealing with racial harassment in each of these circumstances. It should be remembered that not every tenure category was applicable to every respondent: for example, many landlords do not have shared ownership tenancies or properties leased from the private sector.

15.6 The figure nevertheless suggests that policies in respect of secure or assured tenancies are still very much more widespread than policies in the other tenure categories. All the local housing authorities in the survey had secure tenants and nearly all had RTB leaseholders, yet 88 per cent applied their racial harassment polices to the former and only 31 per cent to the latter. An even lower proportion (22 per cent) had extended their policies to the private sector generally. Nearly half the London borough respondents had policies or procedures in respect of RTB leaseholders, compared with just over one in four local authorities elsewhere.

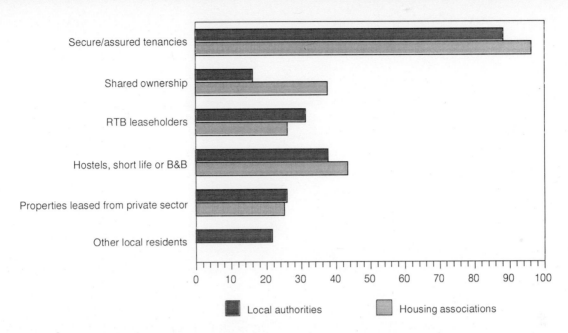

Figure 1   Percentage of respondents with written policies and procedures for racial harassment in the tenure categories shown

Local authorities   Housing associations

Base: 93 LAs and 104 HA respondents to full questionnaire

15.7 Local authority respondents in London and the South East were more likely to have policies and procedures covering temporary accommodation than authorities in other parts of the country. For example, around two thirds had a policy covering hostels and B&B, compared with one in five elsewhere. These differences probably reflect the more widespread use of temporary accommodation in these areas.

15.8 The 57 landlords with ten or more reported incidents in their own stock in the previous year were more likely to have specific policies covering each of the other tenure categories. This was particularly true of hostels, short life and B&B, where 60 per cent had a policy.

Ethnic records

15.9 Another set of questions in the 1991 survey dealt with the extent of ethnic record keeping by local authorities – something that is widely regarded as good practice in multi ethnic areas. As the survey report stated, 'ethnic record keeping is essential both for monitoring allocations and for keeping track of the number of incidents of racial violence and harassment'.

15.10 In 1991, over one fifth of the local authorities completing the full questionnaire kept no ethnic records at all. The corresponding figure in 1994 was just 2 per cent, with a further 2 per cent omitting this series of questions. 88 per cent stated that they were now keeping ethnic records on all new applicants for housing, compared with about half in 1991.

Table 7 Percentage of landlords keeping ethnic records, 1994			
	LAs	HAs	All landlords
New applicants for housing	88	96	92
Existing tenants	19	45	33
Victims of racial harassment	77	78	78

Base: 93 LAs and 104 HAs completing the full questionnaire

15.11 Rather surprisingly, over one in five of the 1994 respondents (both local authorities and housing associations) still do not keep ethnic records on the victims of racial harassment.

15.12 The report of the 1991 survey noted that lack of information on existing tenants was a major shortcoming. Just 11 per cent of the local authority respondents had this information at that time. The proportion in 1994 was 19 per cent – still a low figure compared with the 45 per cent of housing associations who said they had this information. Many associations do have an in-built advantage over local authorities: the rapid expansion of the housing association movement over the last 10-15 years means that many of the associations that have been monitoring their lettings during this time will by now have ethnic origin information on a significant proportion of their tenants. The only other way for either type of landlord to obtain the information is to carry out a tenant census – although local authorities will have been able to obtain aggregate information from the 1991 Population Census.

15.13 It is important to realise that the relatively high level of ethnic record keeping amongst local authority respondents to the full questionnaire will not be typical of local authorities as a whole. The 142 local authorities that responded to the survey by saying that they had no experience or polices in respect of racial harassment are very unlikely to have any form of record-keeping. The extent of record keeping amongst housing associations is likely to be much higher because of the requirements of the Housing Corporation and the need to keep ethnic records for the continuous monitoring of housing association lettings (CORE). Finally, it is worth repeating the usual caveat that keeping ethnic records and using them are two different things.

15.14 All but one of the 57 landlords with 10 or more incidents of racial harassment in the previous year were recording the ethnic origin of all new housing applicants, and of victims of racial harassment. They were also more likely than other landlords to know the ethnic origin of all their tenants – though this still applied to little more than a third of their number (21 in total).

Prevention of racial harassment

15.15 Some respondents pointed out that prevention of racial harassment is the only ultimate 'success'. A successful prosecution or a genuine expression of remorse on the part of a perpetrator is no substitute for a situation in which harassment does not happen in the first place.

15.16 The methods that might be used by a social landlord to prevent harassment include publicising their policies to tenants – in the hope of deterring potential perpetrators – and making sure that potential victims know how to report incidents and what steps the landlord will take in response. Landlords can also use the influence they have with tenants' associations to try to ensure that the latter adopt policies against racial violence and harassment. The stance taken by an active TA can make the difference between an estate where other tenants collude with harassment or affect not to be aware of it, and one where people experiencing harassment are supported and perpetrators made to feel unwelcome. Allied to working with TAs is the community development approach to prevention: this might take the form, for example, of working with any teenage groups that are known to be responsible for racial incidents on an estate. Finally, landlords can put a clause into the tenancy agreement: this serves to increase awareness of their policies and may assist with possession proceedings should the need arise (see Chapter 6).

15.17 Figure 2 shows the percentage of respondents to the full questionnaire that had taken various measures that might fall under the heading of prevention.

Figure 2   Percentage of landlords taking various actions to prevent racial harassment

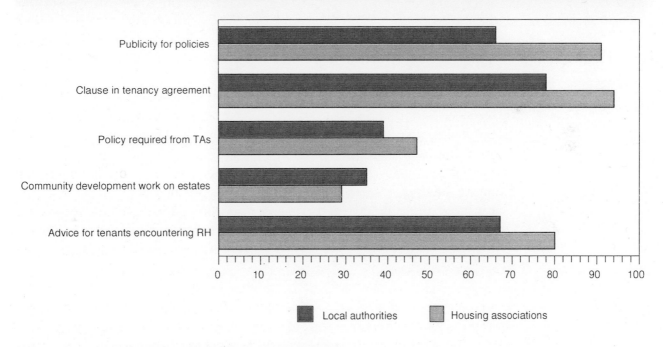

Base: 93 LAs and 104 HAs completing the full questionnaire

15.18 Every housing association had taken at least one of the measures listed on the questionnaire, whereas eight of the 93 local authorities (mainly the ones without written policies on racial harassment) had taken none of these steps.

15.19 At least 33 landlords in the survey (25 LAs and 8 HAs) had policies which had not been publicised amongst their tenants. Nevertheless, the proportion of local authority respondents with publicised policies has risen compared with the previous survey (54 per cent in 1991, 66 per cent in 1994). Comparing answers given by individual local authorities to the same question in 1991 and 1994, 15 of the 20 that had not publicised their policies in 1991 were now doing so. The methods used included sections in tenant handbooks, regular articles in newsletters, and leaflet or poster campaigns. The housing associations operating in some areas had pooled resources to produce joint publicity materials.

15.20 The insertion of a clause on racial harassment into tenancy agreements seems to be the most popular preventative measure with both local authorities and housing associations. Several of the landlords that did not have such clauses at the time of the survey said that they had the matter under consideration. Again, the proportion of LAs taking this measure has increased (61 per cent in 1991, 78 per cent in 1994). Of the 15 local authorities with no clause in 1991 who also answered the question in 1994, 14 now had clauses.

15.21 In each case, a higher proportion of London boroughs and metropolitan authorities had adopted the policy than district councils.

15.22 With the exception of community development work, housing associations were more likely to have adopted each of the measures on the list than local authorities. Housing authorities are (arguably) in a better position to promote community development work, since they can call on the assistance of other local authority departments such as education and social services. However, this may be easier for a unitary authority such as a London borough, than for a district council that is not responsible for all services. 35 per cent of LA respondents had undertaken this type of work in 1994 compared with 28 per cent in 1991.

15.23 Fewer than half the landlords in the survey require tenants' associations to adopt policies against racial violence and harassment, with the local authority percentage increasing from 27 per cent in 1991 to 39 per cent in 1994. This ties in with the findings in chapter 16 of this report which indicate that tenants' and residents' associations are unlikely to be informed about incidents of racial harassment or drawn into multi-agency arrangements.

15.24 All the 57 landlords that had recorded ten or more incidents in the previous year had taken some preventative measures. Over 90 per cent publicised their policies, advised tenants of their procedures and had inserted a clause into their tenancy agreement. Over half had undertaken community development work and had required tenants' associations to adopt anti racial harassment policies. 12 of the 15 housing associations had taken the latter step, however, compared with only 21 of the 42 local authorities.

15.25 Other examples of direct preventative work included a local authority working closely with the police to target problem areas with high profile policing; and another LA organising regular meetings with community groups in such areas.

'Some would argue that real improvement will only occur through a strategy of prevention based on combating racism and racist attitudes more generally. We accept the importance of combating the attitudes and situations which give rise to racial attacks. But such attitudes cannot easily or quickly be changed, and *ethnic minorities need protection now* .... There are no simple or easy solutions, but recent developments and growing awareness of the problem indicate that the potential exists for a much more effective response.' (Home Affairs Committee, 1986).

15.26 The next three chapters consider three important elements of that response: working with other agencies; supporting those experiencing harassment; and dealing with perpetrators.

16   Working with other agencies

16.1 One area the questionnaire examined in detail was the extent to which social landlords were involved in co-operating with other agencies in order to tackle racial violence and harassment. A number of dimensions were looked at, including the exchange of information and any associated difficulties, and social landlords' participation in multi-agency groups.

Providing information to others

16.2 Landlords were asked about the extent to which they provide and receive information on racial attacks, with a distinction being made between individual attacks and statistics on the level of attacks and harassment.

16.3 Informing others within and outside the organisation about individual racial attacks seems to be a well established practice among virtually all LA housing departments and housing associations. There was, however, wide variation as to who is informed, as is illustrated in figure 3.

Figure 3   Percentage of landlords who usually informed the following organisations about individual racial attacks

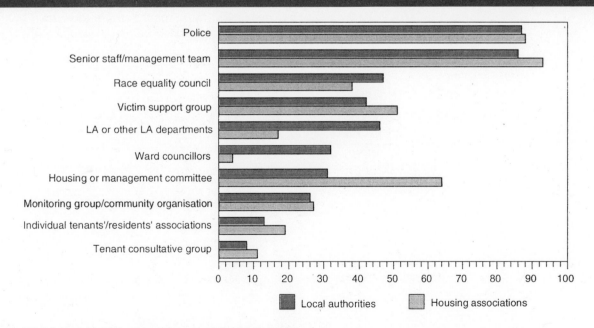

Base: 93 LA and 104 HA respondents to full questionnaire.
Note: the question asked respondents to assume that the victim had consented to others being informed.

16.4 More than four fifths of the LAs and HAs usually informed their senior staff or management team and the police, with over 60 per cent of the HAs also informing their management committee. On the other hand, less than half of social landlords overall indicated that they give this type of information to the local racial equality council or to other organisations directly involved in supporting victims and monitoring racial violence. Those least likely to be informed by either type of landlord were tenants' and residents' groups.

16.5 Social landlords who have to deal regularly with racial incidents (ie those with 10 or more incidents in the previous year) were generally more likely to inform other organisations about individual attacks. This is probably connected with the fact that they are also more likely to be involved in a multi-agency group (see below). One feature of multi-agency working is that information is often circulated to all members of the group. Even so, only a very small minority informed tenants' or residents' groups.

16.6 Given the importance of internal senior staff and the police in responding to incidents of racial violence, it is to be expected that they are the ones most often contacted. It also needs to be noted that not every area has local monitoring or support organisations and that information is generally not passed on without the victim's consent. The urgency with which consent is obtained is likely to be more pronounced in relation to organisations that are seen as vital in taking immediate action, such as the police.

16.7 The provision of information about the *level* of racial attacks and harassment is much more limited and tends to be restricted to internal staff and internal committees (see Figure 4). Nearly three quarters of respondents sent regular reports about the level of racial attacks to senior staff and management teams, and 68 per cent to the housing or management committee, but the proportion sending such reports to outside organisations was a quarter or less, depending on the type of organisation involved. Housing associations were less likely than local authorities to send statistical information to other organisations, in line with the fact they are dealing with fewer incidents overall (Chapter 14) and are less likely to be involved in multi-agency groups (see below).

16.8 The local authorities with ten or more incidents in the previous year provided an exception to this picture. More than half of these authorities sent regular reports to the police and the multi-agency group, and nearly half to the local racial equality council.

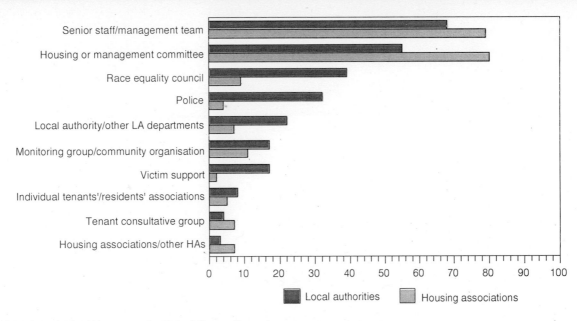

Base: 93 LA and 104 HA respondents to full questionnaire

Receiving information

16.9 The information flow from outside organisations to LA housing departments and housing associations appears to be very limited. This is particularly the case for housing associations, of whom over one third said that they received no information from any outside agency. Where LAs and HAs were given information, it tended to be on individual incidents, and was most often provided by the police.

Figure 5   Percentage of landlords who received information about individual incidents from the organisations listed

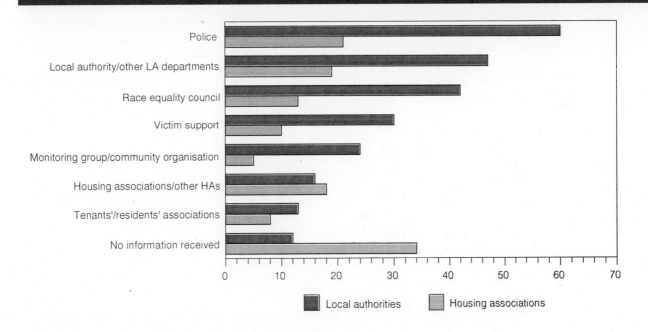

Base: 93 LA and 104 HA respondents to full questionnaire

16.10 Social landlords were even less likely to receive statistical information than notification about individual attacks (just as they themselves were less likely to provide statistics).

Figure 6   Percentage of landlords who received statistical information about racial incidents from the following organisations

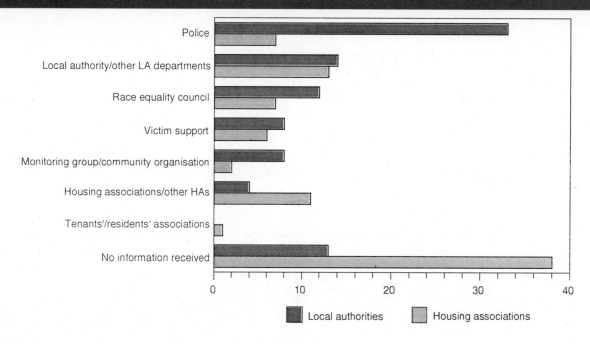

Base: 93 LA and 104 HA respondents to full questionnaire

16.11 The situation among LAs and HAs with ten or more incidents in the previous year was better. Only one respondent in this group said that they never received information from other agencies. But again the proportion of housing associations that receive details of individual incidents or the general level of harassment was lower than for LA housing departments.

16.12 As already indicated, when assessing differences it is important to take into account that not every area has all the types of organisation covered in the questionnaire. However, that appears to be only part of the explanation. The difference between LAs and HAs was also evident where the police were concerned. LA housing departments were much more likely than housing associations to be informed about individual incidents by the police and to be provided with statistics. This difference was just as apparent for landlords that had recorded ten more incidents in the previous year as it was for all landlords in the survey. This suggests that housing associations are not always perceived as key players in tackling or preventing racial violence, and that contacts with other agencies are less well established.

Usefulness of the information received

16.13 Social landlords' views about the usefulness of the information they receive depends on the expectations they have and the purposes for which they want to use the information. It was clear from the responses that these are varied:

- some want to be alerted to any incidents involving their own tenants so that they can begin an immediate investigation;

- some want to be able to track the steps being taken by other agencies and ensure that there is effective victim support or action against the perpetrators;

- others are interested in getting an overall picture, which they can compare with their own records and use in policy development.

16.14 The majority of people found the information they received useful. They felt that it gave them a better overview of the local situation and enabled them to act at an individual or policy level. For instance, various respondents commented that it helped them to provide appropriate support for people experiencing harassment, including necessary evidence to support requests for rehousing. Others pointed out that it helped them to identify high risk areas. This in turn assisted them in decisions about housing allocations to ethnic minorities, housing development proposals or the allocation of resources to support victims and/or prevent racial violence and harassment.

16.15 However, 10 per cent of respondents did not find the information useful. There were various reasons for this: it was late and out of date; difficult to compare because of the lack of standardised report forms; incomplete or inaccurate; or not detailed enough to take action. In this context references were made to the campaigning role of community organisations, the local racial equality council or victim support schemes, and the effect this can have on the accuracy and impartiality of the information provided by such organisations. A few local authorities also made the point that community groups lacked the resources necessary to provide regular and detailed information. As for police statistics, some commented that these sometimes related to a wider area than was useful to social landlords, or did not distinguish between housing-related and other types of racial incident. On the other hand, those more interested in using the information to develop policies felt that the information they received was often too case specific and therefore not useful for policy purposes.

Need for more information

16.16 Nearly half of the social landlords indicated that they would like to get information from agencies with whom they were not currently in contact. Most mentioned the police and LA departments as the agencies they wanted more information from, followed by housing associations and the local racial equality council. However, many had not actually taken any steps to request the information. For those who had, the outcome appeared to be rather disappointing, with most either not having received a response or having been told that the information requested could not be provided.

Obstacles to sharing information

16.17 The majority of landlords said that they did not experience any obstacles to providing information to outside agencies (this question excluded the police). Only 8 per cent felt that there were difficulties – these were mostly linked to the confidential nature of the information.

16.18 The proportion of landlords who indicated that there were obstacles to sharing information with the police was somewhat higher: 20 per cent of all respondents, rising to 33 per cent among LAs and HAs who had ten or more incidents in the previous year. These difficulties arose more often in receiving information from the police than providing it for them. The main obstacles to the latter were confidentiality or the complainant being reluctant to involve the police. One or two housing associations mentioned a reluctance within their own organisation to recognise incidents as racially motivated.

16.19 The failure to recognise incidents as racially motivated was also seen by some as a problem in receiving information *from* the police. More often, however, landlords complained of a slow response from the police, and of information that was difficult to use because of the format or lack of detail. Some landlords stated that delays in getting information from the police were caused by their insistence on the landlord submitting a written request or on the victim signing a consent form before information could be passed on. One HA also reported that they had been charged for police time in connection with possession proceedings against a perpetrator – the police force concerned has since given an undertaking not to charge in these circumstances.

16.20 Many LAs and HAs – particularly those who have to deal with racial incidents on a regular basis – have developed ways of overcoming some of the difficulties in sharing information. The role a multi-agency group plays in this appears to be very important. Examples of good practice most frequently mentioned were the design of a standard report form for collective use and the development of good personal and working relationships with the other agencies. This included:

- regular meetings with the police and racial equality council at which confidential information was discussed;

- a named person at a senior police level who dealt with all requests for information;

- twinning of estate officers with police officers;

- the development of a referral system with the police;

- police attending meetings between landlords and tenants.

16.21 The comments made about exchanging information on racial violence and harassment point to three main issues:

1. Landlords want to be informed about all individual incidents reported to the various agencies. Firstly, because not all tenants who experience racial harassment or violence notify their landlord and without this information landlords are not able to assess the extent of the problem. Secondly, incidents have policy implications for social landlords other than the one directly affected, particularly if they have housing in the localities where

the incidents took place. As one HA pointed out: 'detailed information covering problems in particular areas and estates keeps us aware of the extent of problems that may affect our own dwellings.' For this to happen, the issue of confidentiality needs to be dealt with, though for policy purposes landlords often only want to know about the number of attacks rather than specific details of individual incidents.

2. Given the different ways in which social landlords want to use information about racial violence and harassment, methods of working need to be thought through carefully in order to respond to both casework and strategic needs. One local authority in the survey had established separate internal panels to deal with investigations, monitoring, and appeals. There might be advantages for others in establishing a clearer demarcation between these functions, since they require different kinds of information and (quite probably) different staff input.

3. Comments made about the difficulties in comparing information received from other organisations with that of the social landlords themselves show the need for standard report forms.

Multi-agency groups

16.22 The House of Commons Home Affairs Committee made the following recommendation in 1986:

'All police forces and local authorities whose areas contain an appreciable ethnic minority population should give serious consideration to the establishment of a multi-agency approach to racial incidents, and the Home Office should ensure that knowledge acquired as to the best ways of organising a multi-agency approach is disseminated.'

16.23 The Racial Attacks Group report of 1989 offered guidelines for such work. It recommended that the police and the education, housing and social services departments of the local authority should be involved in any multi-agency initiative, and that they should work closely with the prosecuting authorities and with the legal staff of the local authority. The report also stressed that community and voluntary agencies have a vital role to play.

Involvement in multi-agency working

16.24 Since the 1991 survey, the number of local authority respondents who have a multi-agency group in their area has increased. 70 per cent of the local authorities who completed the full questionnaire said that they had such a group in 1994 compared with 55 per cent in 1991. The proportion for local authorities with ten or more racial incidents in the previous year was even higher, namely 88 per cent. In all, 65 local authorities reported that there were multi-agency groups in their area, compared with 47 in 1991. The inclusion of local authorities whose questionnaires were returned too late for the quantitative analysis suggests that there are currently at least 73 groups in existence. In a small number of cases, however, it appeared that the group covered more than one local authority area, so there may be some duplication in the figures.

16.25 Housing associations seem to be less aware of the existence of multi-agency groups: 33 per cent said they did not know whether there was one in the area where they operated, though this fell to two out of 15 for the associations who recorded ten or more incidents in their housing stock in the previous year. In all, 35 associations (34 per cent of the total HA respondents) had some experience of multi-agency working, some of these in more than one area. Ten of the 15 associations with ten or more incidents the previous year had been involved in multi-agency work.

16.26 Multi-agency groups have become slightly more formalised. Whilst in 1991 61 per cent were formally constituted groups, this has now increased to 65 per cent.

How landlords are represented

16.27 The LAs and HAs who were part of a multi-agency group tended to be represented by more than one person. More than three quarters had senior staff representing them. Among local authorities around one third had an elected member or a chief officer as a representative and 27 per cent a first tier line manager. Front line staff were less likely to be involved. Among housing associations just under one third were represented by a first tier line manager or by front line staff. In some areas housing associations had a collective representative, for instance someone from the local branch of the National Federation of Housing Associations.

16.28 As was noted in the report of the 1991 DoE survey, multi-agency groups consist of a wide range of organisations. Nearly all the groups reported on in this study had representatives from the LA housing department and the police. At least two thirds had representatives from victim support schemes, the local racial equality council, the local education department and social services. Figure 7 shows who were the main agencies represented on 64 multi-agency groups for which local authorities provided details.

Figure 7 Representation on the 64 multi-agency groups for whom details were available from LA respondents

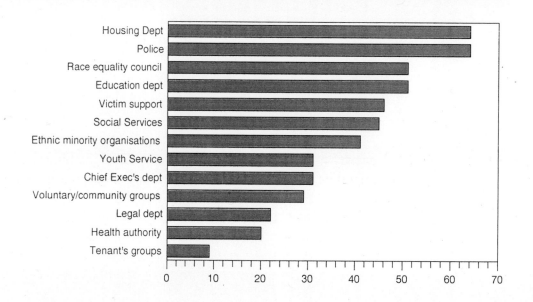

16.29 The first report from the Racial Attacks Group (1989) described the involvement of the police, education, housing and social services departments as 'essential'. It is possible that the apparently better representation of housing departments compared with education and social services is simply a bias in the survey introduced by the fact that the questionnaires were mainly completed by staff in housing departments.

16.30 The lack of involvement of tenant representatives on these groups is very noticeable and their participation rate seems to have declined since the 1991 survey. There has also been no improvement in the representation of local authority legal departments. The 1989 RAG report noted that the 'essential' agencies would 'need to work closely' with the legal officers of the local authority. The representation of legal departments was not much greater in the 42 local authorities that had recorded at least ten incidents in their own housing stock in the previous year: only 17 of these had a legal representative on the multi-agency group.

Activities

16.31 The majority of multi-agency groups were involved in the exchange of information about general trends and in preventative work, including publicity campaigns. In addition, more than half exchanged information about individual cases, co-ordinated action against perpetrators and organised victim support. Perhaps not surprisingly, groups in areas where racial violence and harassment occur more frequently were more involved in preventative work and co-ordinating action to support victims and deal with perpetrators than the multi-agency groups elsewhere.

The benefits of multi-agency working

16.32 Except for a small minority (3 per cent of respondents), working together in a multi-agency group was seen as having a variety of benefits. Over 80 per cent felt that it increased understanding between agencies, and over two thirds that it had led to better co-ordination and had improved the way incidents were recorded and reported. 56 per cent also mentioned the benefit of adopting common definitions of racial violence and harassment and 47 per cent thought that by working together more cases were coming to light.

16.33 On all these criteria, the 35 housing associations were slightly less enthusiastic than the 65 local authorities. The associations with ten or more incidents also perceived the benefits to be more limited than the local authority housing departments. For them the benefits were largely confined to better co-ordination and improvements in recording, and were far less about promoting better understanding between agencies or adopting common definitions.

16.34 This difference was also evident in people's assessment of the effect multi-agency working has on dealing with casework. Ultimately, this is the single most important criterion on which the multi-agency approach can be judged. The majority of respondents thought that cases were tackled more effectively, although again the view was more widespread amongst the local authorities (75 per cent) than the housing associations (60 per cent). In 1991, less than half the local authorities involved in multi-agency groups thought that cases were being tackled more effectively as a result, so there would seem to have been some improvement in their evaluation. Eight out of 13 LAs that had said there was no improvement in the way that cases were dealt with in 1991 now said that multi-agency work was bringing about such an improvement.

16.35 Respondents were asked why they held their particular view on casework. The reasons they gave for a positive view about the effects of multi-agency working on dealing with individual incidents were similar to the general benefits: the most important being better co-ordination and co-operation, being able to share resources, advice and skills, and being able to provide better victim support.

16.36 Those who felt that multi-agency working did not contribute to cases being tackled more effectively attributed this to the lack of commitment of some agencies, the fact that policies decided upon at the multi-agency level are not always communicated downwards to front line staff, and problems with defining racial violence and harassment. One LA commented that multi-agency work in their area lacked direction. There was also a group of respondents who felt that though working in a multi-agency setting provided benefits, there was room for improvement.

Problems with multi-agency working

16.37 Although most respondents felt there were advantages in the multi-agency approach, they also had criticisms. 47 per cent thought that there was a lack of co-operation or commitment from some agencies, whilst 28 per cent felt there were problems in agreeing the role each agency should play and 19 per cent that they had problems with defining racial harassment. 44 per cent quoted problems with the exchange of information. For landlords who had to deal more regularly with racial incidents, lack of co-operation or commitment and problems about agreeing roles were particularly important concerns: 62 per cent mentioned co-operation as a problem; 40 per cent problems with roles. A different but equally important problem was lack of resources, mentioned by 42 per cent. These issues are considered in more detail below.

Exchanging information

16.38 As with sharing information outside the context of multi-agency working, the main problem identified was the reluctance of agencies to provide information because of confidentiality considerations. This applied to both giving information to and getting information from participating agencies. The second most frequently mentioned obstacle was the way racial incidents were monitored and the format used to record them, which often resulted in information that lacked comparability or completeness. Some also commented that not all agencies were fully committed to this way of working and did not give it the priority it deserved. In this context references were made to the different demands and expectations of those involved. There were also various comments about the organisational aspects of a multi-agency group which made it difficult to share information. These included the lack of a clear contact person or the fact that none of the agencies took on a co-ordinating role.

Commitment of other agencies

16.39 The proportion of local authorities complaining about a lack of co-operation or commitment from other agencies has increased since the 1991 survey (57 per cent now compared with 40 per cent then). There is further evidence of what appears to be growing disillusion from the response of the 24 local authorities that replied to the question in both the 1991 and 1994 surveys. In 1991, eight of these authorities said that lack of co-operation or commitment from other agencies was a problem, but in 1994 the number had risen to 17, including 13 that had reported no problems previously.

16.40 The 'other agencies' referred to were likely to include voluntary and community groups as well as the police. A couple of local authority respondents expressed frustration at the apparent unwillingness of the community groups in their areas to get involved in multi-agency working, implying that they preferred to criticise from the sidelines. Other respondents, however, felt that resources were the main obstacle. Some voluntary and community groups were reluctant to take on a victim support role, for example, for fear that they would unable to cope with the numbers needing help.

Definition of racial harassment

16.41 There also appears to have been a lack of progress on the basic issue of agreeing a definition of racial harassment. 21 per cent of local authorities reported that this was a problem in 1991 and 25 per cent in 1994. The definition of a racial incident originally adopted by the Association of Chief Police Officers in 1985 is:

> *any incident in which it appears to the reporting or investigating officer that the complaint involves an element of racial motivation, or any incident which includes an allegation of racial motivation made by any person.*

16.42 This definition has been adopted by all police forces in England and Wales and forms the basis of police statistics. It has also been adopted by the Racial Attacks Group (1989). The second RAG report (1991) stated:

> 'It is recognised that agencies may have their own definitions of racial attacks, but, for the purposes of multi-agency working, the adoption of a common definition is essential. The definition recommended in the (first) RAG report is well suited to this ... . It is based firmly on victim, witness and/or officer perception, and as such, is wide enough to encompass the range of definitions already adopted by individual agencies. The good faith of agencies is called into question if victim's needs remain unmet simply because the agencies cannot agree a form of words.'

16.43 Local authorities and housing associations have long been encouraged to take a victim-centred approach to racial violence and harassment. It is possible that some may have been using similar definitions to that adopted by the CRE in 1987[4]:

---

[4] The CRE has recently published a guide for multi-agency panels which provides a new and updated definition of racial harassment (CRE, 1995). However, the 1987 definition was still in use at the time of the research.

... violence which may be verbal or physical and which includes attacks on property as well as on the person, suffered by individuals or groups because of their colour, race, nationality or ethnic or national origins, when the victim believes that the perpetrator was acting on racial grounds and/or there is evidence of racism.

16.44 The definitions quoted above are similar, although the ACPO/RAG definition is arguably the wider of the two. It is not possible to tell from the questionnaire responses whether such nuances were at the root of the definitional problems experienced by some multi-agency groups, or whether there were other issues at stake. Previous research suggests that whilst definitions may be formally agreed, they are not always applied in practice:

> 'Even at the end of the project there was still disagreement between ground level police and housing officers over whether a given incident was racially motivated, or merely a neighbour dispute.' (Bowling and Saulsbury, 1993).

16.45 A number of new multi-agency groups have formed since the 1991 survey and it is possible to argue that definitions are a common teething problem. However, of the 24 local authorities that answered this question in both questionnaires, the number reporting problems with definitions had actually increased from two to five.

Conclusion

16.46 Two local authorities in the West Midlands provided diametrically opposed views on the value of multi-agency working:

> 'Agencies participating are more aware of each other's activities and ability to provide assistance. A co-ordinated and targeted response is thereby more easily achievable providing, ultimately, a better and more accessible service to victims. Responses/decisions of the multi-agency forum are 'owned' by its members both individually and collectively.'

> 'As the agency is outside the management structure of (the) local police/ local authority, members represent/defend their organisation's interests, which creates lack of ownership, making it ineffective with no real authority in (the) decision making process. It takes longer to deal with individual cases and regards still have to be made to the appropriate organisation to deal with the case.'

16.47 It has to be said that the latter view was in the minority and that few if any of the landlords that were involved in multi-agency working expressed any wish to go back to a single agency approach. Nevertheless, the problems that continue to be experienced by some multi-agency participants – especially lack of commitment from other agencies – are clearly issues that need to be addressed if disillusion with this method of working is not to grow.

17 Supporting those experiencing harassment

17.1 Being on the receiving end of racial violence or harassment is an extremely traumatic experience. Harassment directed at one member of the household has consequences for everybody else. Support for victims is therefore a crucial element when responding to racial incidents. The questionnaire began by exploring a number of elements of victim support:

- whether repairs to the home were carried out within a specified time;

- whether victims were provided with a package of information detailing the support services available locally and the landlord's own procedures on racial harassment;

- whether there was a support or protection scheme for witnesses: this might take the form, for example, of staying overnight before a court appearance, or escorting children to school;

- whether there was a complaints procedure in place should victims feel that they were not receiving sufficient support from their landlord.

17.2 Figure 8 shows how the responses of local authorities and housing associations compared. The majority of landlords, even those who said that they had very few incidents, had developed ways of helping victims. The most common measure was to carry out the necessary repairs to the homes of victims within a clearly defined period of time following the incident. 83 per cent of all landlords and 93 per cent of those with ten or more incidents in the previous year had adopted such a policy.

Figure 8   Percentage of landlords taking various actions to support victims

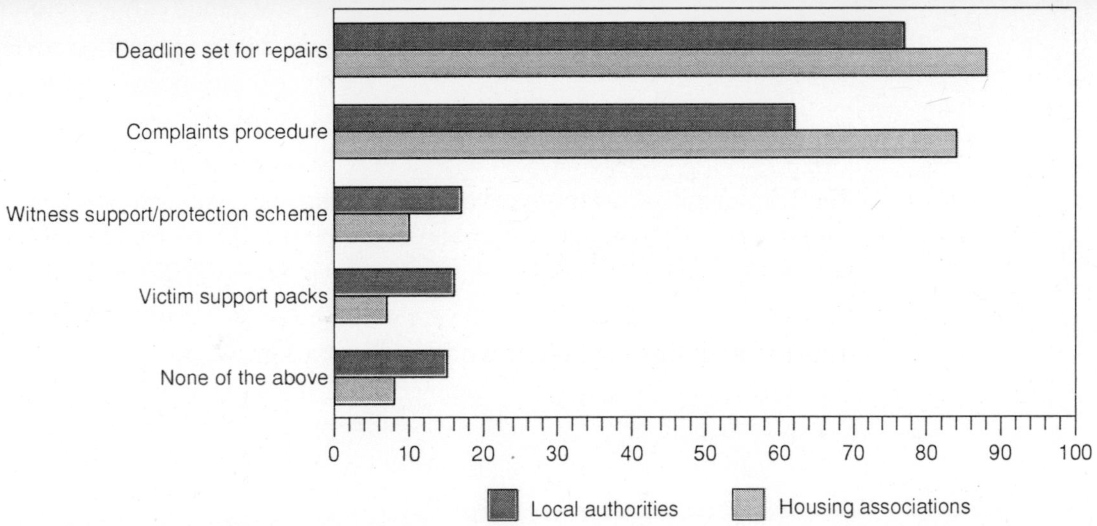

Base: 93 LA and 104 HA respondents to full questionnaire

17.3 Complaints procedures for victims who feel that they have not received adequate support were also widespread: 74 per cent of all landlords operated such procedures, but they were more common amongst housing associations than local authorities.

17.4 Witness support schemes and victim support packs were less common, even among the more experienced landlords (30 per cent and 26 per cent, respectively).

17.5 If people experiencing racial harassment are to get the best support available in a locality, it is obviously important that they are informed about the various support and advice services on offer. 80 per cent of all landlords, and 91 per cent of those who had recorded ten or more incidents in the previous year, indicated that they did this. Housing associations were slightly more active in this respect than local authority housing departments.

17.6 It was not always clear from the descriptions given whether housing staff were actively involved in putting victims and support agencies in touch with each other. The most common practice seems to be for staff to hand over leaflets or a victim support pack – or to tell complainants about the services and local support groups available – during either the first interview or (less frequently) when making a home visit. The decision whether to contact any of the agencies is then left to the victims themselves. In a minority of cases respondents mentioned that housing staff contacted agencies on victims' behalf.

17.7 Respondents were also asked to give their own examples of good practice. 38 per cent of all respondents and 60 per cent of those who had 10 or more incidents provided such examples. They revealed a wide range of approaches used by social landlords to try and respond appropriately to racial incidents.

17.8 The most common examples involved the use of translators and interpreters in order to ensure good communication with people experiencing harassment. Various landlords recognised that ethnic origin and gender of the investigating officer can influence the interviews and, where possible, matched the ethnic origin and/or gender of staff with that of the victim. Others used joint visits (by, for example, the police and a housing officer, or a housing officer and community worker or member of a local community group) in order to make the first interview non-threatening for the victim. Some provided dictaphones to ensure that the complainant had the opportunity to describe the incident in detail.

17.9 Respondents also gave examples of follow-up support. This included very practical help, such as installing a direct line to an emergency support centre, connecting people to a community alarm system, financial help with telephone bills, and monitoring the situation by asking victims to keep daily records using a diary or a dictaphone, or through regular visits. Giving complainants information about other support agencies, arranging counselling, and liaising with victim support services were also mentioned. Some commented that they used the same member of staff throughout to provide continuity in the relationship with the person experiencing harassment.

Communication with potential victims

17.10 Some approaches were intended to encourage people experiencing racial harassment to come forward. In many instances this involved multi lingual publicity about the landlord's policy and procedure on racial violence and harassment, and about advice and support services. As mentioned in Chapter 15, some housing associations had pooled resources in order to produce publicity material. Some areas had, as part of multi-agency co-operation, established a 24 hour helpline, or were considering a racial harassment centre offering advice and help in different languages. There were also landlords who held regular surgeries or consultation meetings with local community groups in localities with persistent harassment problems.

Improving organisational responses

17.11 A number of the initiatives described were concerned with improving the way the housing department or the association responded to racial incidents. Some were aimed at improving good practice through the development of a staff manual on the organisation's policy and procedures and through training staff on how to deal with racial incidents, how to interview victims and how to use interpreters. Others were concerned with extending the service by appointing or part-funding racial harassment workers or taking on staff with the necessary language skills; or by developing community based resources – for instance, training community organisations to provide victim support or training people to become interpreters. One or two landlords also mentioned that they had put internal mechanisms in place to ensure priority action whenever an incident of racial violence occurred.

Successes in helping victims

17.12 A combination of lack of experience and reticence about claiming 'success' meant that only 40 per cent of respondents gave examples of successful ways of helping victims of racial harassment. Furthermore, there was an overlap between examples of good practice in communicating with victims and those identified as successful victim support.

Working alone

17.13 By far the most common example of successful support mentioned was the provision of alternative accommodation, although quite a number of respondents were apologetic about having had to rehouse victims, commenting that this was 'not altogether a success', and stressing that it was always at the victim's request.

17.14 Various respondents also referred to ways of protecting people against further attacks whilst remaining in their present home, by installing security measures such as alarm systems, fireproof letterboxes, improved locks and lighting. One LA had installed micro closed circuit TV to monitor the victim's front door. Several landlords had linked victims to alarm systems normally used for elderly tenants. Telephone hotlines included one system where at the press of a button the victim would be connected to the housing department, whose operator had the address on computer and a direct line to Scotland Yard.

17.15 Some landlords mentioned that they paid for legal advice, counselling, temporary accommodation costs, or removal expenses. One housing association had helped a tenant overturn an injunction obtained by a perpetrator.

17.16 A number of respondents commented that their support for those experiencing racial harassment had had a positive effect at a broader level. By providing good support they had prevented some estates becoming 'no go areas', or had improved liaison with ethnic minority groups.

Working with others

17.17 Rehousing of victims was also given as an example of successful collaboration with other agencies. This was particularly so for housing associations. In such instances, LAs and HAs use nomination, mobility and exchange arrangements to help people who want to move to a different area. LAs had also assisted a number of HAs by arranging emergency temporary accommodation, for instance where a victim was unwilling to return home. A few landlords had worked together to ensure that they did not unknowingly rehouse each other's perpetrators.

17.18 Agencies also worked together to provide victim support. Successful initiatives here were most frequently mentioned by local authorities. More generally, successful collaboration was defined by some respondents as being able to access specialist skills or resources not available within their own organisation.

18   Dealing with perpetrators

'We believe that a more pro-active stance should be taken towards the perpetrators of racial harassment, with the presumption in favour of eviction of repeated offenders...' (Home Affairs Committee, 1994)

18.1 This chapter reviews the actions taken by social landlords when dealing with perpetrators whose identity is known. Some of the measures taken in cases where the identity of perpetrators is unknown fall under the heading of prevention (see Chapter 15) as do the more general publicity and awareness campaigns by which social landlords seek to deter potential perpetrators before the event.

Background

18.2 Racial harassment is not a specific offence in criminal law or a ground for the eviction of a secure tenant. However, the behaviour involved can lead to prosecution or eviction on a number of other grounds. The Criminal Justice and Public Order Act of 1994, for example, introduced a new offence of intentional harassment.

18.3 Until 1988, both local authorities and housing associations granted secure tenancies. Since 1988, most new housing association tenancies have been assured tenancies. The grounds on which possession proceedings are likely to be brought against perpetrators of racial harassment are very similar, however, for both types of tenancy. Schedule 2 of the Housing Act 1985 (secure tenancies) and Schedule 2 of the Housing Act 1988 (assured tenancies) provide three very similar grounds on which the courts may grant possession:

- if any obligation of the tenancy has been broken or not performed;

- if the tenant or anyone residing with him/her has caused nuisance or annoyance to neighbours;

- if there has been deterioration due to 'acts of waste', such as writing graffiti in communal areas.

18.4 The first ground provides a clear incentive to social landlords to make sure that there is a clause covering racial harassment in their tenancy agreements. The second ground will be extended in significant ways if the housing bill before Parliament in early 1996 is enacted (see section 10 of the good practice review).

18.5 The courts are not *obliged* to grant a possession order in the above circumstances, even if the tenant is in clear breach of the agreement or 'nuisance and annoyance' is proved or admitted. They consider whether or not it is *reasonable* to make an order, taking into account, for example, the tenants' personal circumstances.

18.6 Legal action by social landlords need not, of course, be restricted to possession proceedings. Guidance written for local authorities (eg Forbes, 1988) has drawn attention to the wide range of remedies that are potentially available under both civil and criminal law – many of which can also be applied by housing associations. In recent years some landlords have made increasing use of injunctions. These can be used to prevent a breach of the tenancy agreement or to prevent nuisance or trespass; and they can be obtained quickly and without witnesses having to attend court. Restrictive covenants in freehold conveyances or in the lease of flats can be used against all future owners of properties that have been sold under Right to Buy or shared ownership arrangements.

Action taken by landlords

18.7 Figure 9 shows the percentage of landlords responding to the full questionnaire that had taken various types of action. In contrast to the question on preventative measures, local authorities were rather more likely than housing associations to have taken most of the steps shown. 11 per cent of local authorities and 13 per cent of housing associations had not taken any of the actions against perpetrators on the list.

Figure 9   Percentage of social landlords that had taken each type of action against perpetrators

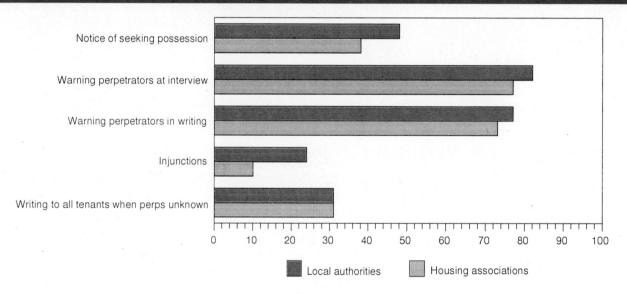

Base: 93 LA and 104 HA respondents to the full questionnaire

18.8 It should be noted that the question asked if landlords had actually dealt with perpetrators in the ways shown – not if they had a policy to do so. This was a change in the form of the question asked in the 1991 questionnaire, so the results for this question are not strictly comparable with the previous survey. The more incidents that are reported to landlords, the greater the chance that the identity of some of the perpetrators is known, and that some witnesses will be willing to give evidence. It is possible, therefore, that local authorities appear to have been more energetic in taking legal action against perpetrators simply because they have more experience of racial harassment (see chapter 14). Over two thirds of the landlords with ten or more reported cases of harassment in the previous year had issued NOSPs.

18.9 Both LAs and HAs were much more likely to have interviewed perpetrators and/or written to them about the alleged harassment than they were to have taken legal action – although nearly half the local authorities had got as far as issuing Notices of Seeking Possession (NOSPs). A much lower proportion had taken out injunctions, even though experience suggests that these are somewhat easier to obtain than possession orders. Nearly half of the local authorities with ten or more reported incidents in the previous year had used injunctions, but only two of the 15 housing associations.

18.10 Turning to the local authorities that answered this series of questions in both 1991 and 1994, ten of the 27 that did not have a *policy* of taking out injunctions in 1991 had started to issue them by 1994. However, eight of the 12 who said they *did* have such a policy in 1991 had not taken out any injunctions by 1994.

18.11 There is a similar pattern of mixed progress in respect of NOSPs. Nine of the 17 local authorities that did not have a *policy* of issuing NOSPs in 1991 had issued some by 1994. On the other hand, five of the 22 that said they *did* have a policy in 1991 had still not issued an NOSP three years later.

18.12 As far as local authorities were concerned, the highest proportion of respondents taking each kind of action was found amongst the London boroughs, and the lowest proportion amongst the non metropolitan authorities.

Possession proceedings

18.13 The 85 landlords that had issued NOSPs by 1994 were asked to state *how many* had been issued in the most recent year (1993 or 1993/94). Of the 74 that answered the question, 27 had issued none in that year and 33 had issued just one or two. One local authority had issued 15, and another 14. None of the other landlords had issued more than six.

18.14 Comparing the local authority responses with the 1991 questionnaire, there is some evidence of increasing activity. In 1991, 21 local authorities had issued a total of 94 NOSPs over whatever time period had elapsed since they first adopted this policy. In 1994, the number of authorities that had ever issued NOSPs had risen to 45, 27 of whom had issued a total of 93 NOSPs in the most recent year.

18.15 Table 8 shows what happened to the notices that had been issued in 1993 or 1993/94:

Table 8 NOSPs in 1993 or 1993/94	LAs	HAs	Total
Number issued	93	36	130
Taken to court	22	4	26
Granted immediate possession	5	0	5
Granted suspended possession	2	1	3
Evicted	9	1	10
Cases not proven	2	0	2

18.16 It is difficult to collect accurate information in this area because of the time taken for cases to be resolved. LAs, for example, may have reported the number of evictions that took place in 1993 or 1993/94 rather than number of NOSPs issued in those years that subsequently resulted in eviction. In some cases, the outcome of the case was still not known at the time of the survey. Nevertheless, the figures do suggest that only a very small proportion of NOSPs proceed to a possession order and eviction.

18.17 Social landlords are often criticised for what appears to be an extremely high rate of attrition. They investigate many cases of racial harassment, but institute few legal proceedings. When NOSP proceedings are commenced, very few seem to result in the eventual eviction of perpetrators. In their defence, landlords often point out the difficulties they face in identifying perpetrators, obtaining evidence to a standard that is likely to satisfy the courts, and persuading victims or other witnesses to testify when they may be facing threats or intimidation. Taking a victim-centred approach may mean that a potentially good case is never developed, because the person experiencing the harassment does not want legal action. The Home Affairs Committee first considered this issue in 1989, when just three evictions were known to have ever taken place for this reason in local authority housing. The DoE had informed them of three main problems:

> '... the reluctance of witnesses, the difficulties in court proceedings for eviction and difficulties in the approach and preparedness of local authorities. Some housing departments have not undertaken full and early liaison with legal departments and the police; some officers concerned in the collection of evidence lack sufficient training, and a large number of local authorities do not yet include a specific anti-harassment clause in their tenancy agreements, which can serve to back up an eviction case in court. We re-emphasise the Committee's original recommendation and we expect these difficulties to be overcome ...'

18.18 The current research has already suggested that the last point – the lack of a clause in tenancy agreements – has now largely been addressed by local authorities (and to an even greater extent by housing associations). This research was not designed to test the liaison between housing and legal departments, but previous research in this area has spoken of 'a vicious circle of inaction' in which housing departments, deterred by what they feel to be a lack of support and advice from legal officers, fail to refer cases where legal action would clearly be appropriate:

> 'A lack of professional trust can contribute to a situation in which housing officers, although they often have the responsibility under racial harassment procedures for initially seeking advice on cases, actually give far greater priority themselves to other solutions, such as housing transfers for victims, which are seen as lying within their own professional and departmental prerogative ..... while housing departments made regular complaints about the service provided by their legal departments, it was clear that they actually made very infrequent use of them. Moreover, when they did, the case had often been in progress for many weeks and had become stale. Both injunctions and possession actions are severely prejudiced by such delays and, as a result, a potentially strong case can be turned into a weak one, thereby leading to negative legal advice'. (Legal Action Group, 1990).

18.19 A few local authorities in the survey had 'dedicated' legal staff who worked full time on racial harassment cases. This offers one way of overcoming the problems described above for those landlords with a sufficient volume of work. Other HAs and LAs were engaging local solicitors with experience of this type of work.

Interviewing perpetrators

18.20 Responses to the open-ended questions, however, suggested that there is an additional reason for the low eviction rate: it is not unusual for the warnings to work. When asked to say what successes they had had in dealing with perpetrators, 44 per cent of LAs and 32 per cent of HAs offered examples: a total of 74 landlords. The most frequent reference (made by half these landlords) was to harassment stopping after a warning had been issued. 40 per cent mentioned some form of legal action (NOSPs, injunctions, prosecutions) but only 17 per cent mentioned eviction – another reflection, perhaps, of the small number of landlords that have pursued cases this far.

18.21 Many respondents stated that warning perpetrators about the possible consequences of their actions had caused the behaviour to stop. This point was made by landlords with extensive experience of dealing with racial harassment as well as those with just a handful of cases, although the former stressed that it did not always work, and that now and again it was actually counter-productive. One local authority gave the following examples:

'Victim complained of verbal abuse following dispute over car parking. Perpetrator visited by Housing Officer, warned about behaviour. Perpetrator subsequently apologised and relationship restored'.

'Following an incident of name calling and objects being thrown at door a joint visit was made to perpetrators by Housing Services and Police. Parents of child perpetrators subsequently apologised for behaviour of children'.

18.22 Even if the perpetrator does not respond to the initial warning from the landlord, there is still a chance that he or she will give an undertaking not to repeat the behaviour once legal proceedings have started.

18.23 It is impossible to tell from a postal questionnaire whether landlords were always right in their assessment of the effectiveness of interviews and warning letters, although there is some support for their view in recent Home Office research (1995). It may be that in some cases the harassment continues, unbeknown to the landlord, because the victim tires of making reports when nothing appears to be done, or because they feel too threatened and unprotected by the authorities to risk making further reports. Landlords certainly vary in the thoroughness with which they follow up previous cases and check with victims that there really has been no recurrence.

18.24 Nevertheless, the claims made by social landlords that many perpetrators do stop deserve to be taken seriously. This is, after all, what many victims would want more than anything else: that the harassment should simply cease, without the stress of a court appearance and the risk of escalation or revenge attacks. Well-conducted interviews with perpetrators by well trained staff can be effective. Useful guidance for housing managers on this topic was published by Lemos Associates in 1993. The general approach is reflected in the comments of a co-operative housing association:

'The initial meeting with the perpetrator is important for it to be productive. Therefore people conducting the meeting should meet with their line manager before the interview and consider how they are going to handle various scenarios that might arise. There are certain predictable patterns, ie denial, blame someone else, counter accusation, blame the victim etc. Normally, perpetrators are informed that there has been a complaint, explain the co-op's policy and procedure on racial harassment, inform them how seriously the organisation takes harassment and what potential consequences are for them, discourage them from abuse and attacks. Above all, purpose of the visit is to STOP THE HARASSMENT'.

18.25 A number of landlords stated that perpetrators had left of their own accord following warnings or possession proceedings, and in a few cases the landlord had agreed to transfer them.

Other work with perpetrators

18.26 Successful efforts to gather evidence (mentioned by much smaller numbers of landlords) included the use of surveillance cameras, private investigators and professional witnesses.

18.27 A few landlords favoured a more conciliatory approach to perpetrators and had either attempted to mediate between the parties themselves, or had engaged professional mediation services. It was not always possible to tell from their responses why they thought this course of action was appropriate. In at least one case the LA concerned felt it was a way of tackling problems before they escalated and that it provided a means of stopping the harassment without putting victims through the stress of court appearances. Elsewhere it appeared that landlords were offering mediation in cases which they interpreted as neighbour disputes, albeit with racial overtones. One LA had deliberately avoided mediation, since this could be seen to 'validate racism', but they too emphasised the need for early identification of the problem and action to stop it escalating. They felt this had helped them avoid the growth of no-go areas.

18.28 Other ways of working with perpetrators included encouraging youth activities, trying to improve awareness and tackle 'ignorance', and arranging help for perpetrators with mental health problems. Generating 'peer pressure' and involving tenants' associations were also mentioned. However, these measures were quoted by far fewer landlords than interviewing or sending warning letters to perpetrators, supplemented by legal action when required.

Working with other agencies

18.29 Asked about successes they had had working with other agencies in dealing with perpetrators, only 43 landlords (27 LAs and 16 HAs) gave examples. 18 of these specifically mentioned co-operation with the police, whilst 11 mentioned more than one agency or a multi-agency group. Only two landlords (both local authorities) mentioned any successes in gaining the co-operation of tenants' or residents' associations.

18.30 The kind of assistance obtained included surveillance and gathering evidence, making joint visits to warn perpetrators, and prosecutions. 20 local authorities mentioned this kind of assistance, compared with 9 housing associations.

Attitudes of the courts

18.31 Of the 197 local authorities and housing associations that completed the full questionnaire, only 19 had sufficient experience of the courts to feel in a position to comment on how the courts deal with possession cases. Most were local authorities and their views were rather mixed. Some commented that the court had been sympathetic and helpful. The specific points made were that the judge recognised that racial harassment was a serious issue, or was sympathetic towards the victim and supportive of action against the perpetrator. One respondent recalled a court case where the judge recommended a more effective wording to an injunction and adjourned for 30 minutes to permit new documentation to be prepared.

18.32 Others emphasised that they had not found the court to be understanding. Complaints included the judge showing a lack of respect for witnesses, holding the view that eviction of perpetrators would increase youth homelessness, and a general lack of awareness about racial harassment. One LA was dismayed to hear an alleged perpetrator described as a 'good tenant'.

18.33 One or two respondents felt that the courts were impeded by the lack of any specific law on racial harassment. Another view, expressed several times, was that the court can only help when the evidence meets all the necessary (and stringent) requirements. As one housing association commented:

> 'Courts require a very high standard of evidence and this has proved difficult to meet. Also compiling evidence to this standard has proved extremely time consuming and very costly (eg in one case legal fees came to approximately £14,000 and we were unable to obtain the eviction of the perpetrator).'

18.34 There was also a feeling that racial harassment cases are too often treated as a breach of peace or vandalism.

Communicating success

18.35 Successful action against perpetrators can contribute to the prevention of future attacks. The Racial Attacks Group also wished to know whether landlords were communicating information about successful cases to their other tenants and to members of the public. 31 landlords (25 local authorities and six housing associations) said that they had done this. 22 had used the methods by which they would normally communicate with tenants: newsletters, annual reports, tenants' handbooks etc. 12 landlords (all local authorities) had contacted the media and obtained coverage in the local press or radio. A smaller number of local authorities had held public meetings or organised a conference.

18.36 It is inherently difficult for social landlords to assess the impact of publicity in such circumstances. It is fairly obvious when publicity backfires (for example if the family being harassed is named in media reports and is subsequently subjected to further harassment – as happened in the case of one respondent). It is much harder – if not impossible – to detect how often the knowledge that someone else has been evicted or prosecuted may have deterred potential perpetrators. Of the landlords in the survey who attempted an answer to this question (all of whom were local authorities) 15 felt the publicity had had an impact, four felt it had had no impact and eight were not sure.

18.37 According to these respondents, the positive effects of publicity about 'successful' cases include the following:

- some perpetrators are deterred;

- victims and potential victims feel reassured that something is being done;

- the incidence of harassment falls;

- reported incidents rise (because victims are more willing to come forward);

- landlords are able to demonstrate their commitment – eg to community leaders or their own staff.

19 Carrying out surveys

Existence of local surveys

19.1 Twenty five LAs and 18 HAs said they were aware of local surveys on victims of racial incidents, though a number of landlords pointed out that they insert questions about racial harassment in their annual tenants' surveys. As is to be expected, it was the landlords with most experience of racial violence who were most aware of locally conducted studies.

19.2 The majority of the surveys that respondents knew about had been completed by the local authority housing department, again not surprisingly, given the financial resources necessary to carry out a survey and the role of local authorities as providers of social housing. The limited number of in-house studies among housing associations may explain why HA respondents were more aware of surveys carried out by other agencies than local authority respondents.

19.3 Those who knew of local surveys were asked to provide further details. Only a small minority did so. Examples of surveys that were specifically designed to collect information about racial harassment included:

- an interview survey of 41 households who had reported incidents, which aimed to find out about their support needs, their views of the housing department response, and the physical and psychological effects of the harassment;

- an interview survey designed to measure the extent of racial harassment, the level of reporting, and satisfaction with the response of various agencies. A control survey was subsequently undertaken with white households;

- a postal survey of ethnic minority tenants in a London borough which aimed to uncover the extent of harassment.

Use of survey findings

19.4 One of the reasons for asking about local studies was to assess whether social landlords use the results of such studies to inform their policies and practice. Over half of the 43 respondents, including nearly all those with ten or more incidents in the previous year, indicated that their organisation had discussed the findings. Around half said that the surveys had an effect on their work. Improvements in service delivery were most frequently mentioned. This ranged from developing clearer policies and procedures to a better co-ordination of action towards victims and perpetrators, and extending the service available. For instance, one LA decided on the basis of survey findings to seek funding for posts under section 11 of the Local Government Act 1966 (section 11 is concerned with the provision of specialist staff where there are significant numbers of ethnic minorities with different languages or customs; some of the budget for s.11 has now been transferred to the Single Regeneration Budget).

19.5   Others had used the results in staff training programmes or in raising awareness more generally. But surveys also had the function of informing social landlords about specific aspects of racial violence and harassment. For example, one HA reported that a local survey had alerted them to the activities of racist organisations in one of its areas.

Need for survey advice

19.6   Surveys seem to be perceived as a useful tool in gaining a better understanding of the problem and the role of service providers; 85 per cent of all LAs and HAs, and 90 per cent of those with more experience of racial incidents said that written guidelines on how to carry out a survey would be helpful[5]. Respondents were most interested in advice on how to find out about the support needs of victims or how to evaluate the service they provided, but over two thirds were also interested in ways of measuring the extent of the problem in their area.

19.7   Those with more experience of dealing with racial incidents, and, therefore, more familiar with the needs of victims, were most interested in guidance on how to evaluate service provision. However, the comments of a few respondents also suggest a need for very practical advice: for instance how to provide effective support, how to develop community initiatives and how to involve other agencies. With respect to the latter, the study found some evidence that the lack of involvement by community groups is causing concern.

Other feedback methods

19.8   Surveys are only one way of gauging people's experience of racial violence and harassment and their views of the services provided. The questionnaire also explored whether landlords had used other approaches to get feedback from victims. Only 13 per cent of housing association respondents and 20 per cent of local authorities had done so. One in three landlords with ten or more incidents indicated that they had tried to get feedback by methods other than surveys.

19.9   The most common way to find out about the experiences of victims involved monitoring through regular follow up visits, the use of a telephone hotline and through diaries. Other methods were more collective in nature and included group discussions with tenants, conferences and public enquiries. Regular contact with victim support groups, community leaders, the local racial equality council or local monitoring groups were also mentioned. One or two respondents said they used the local radio.

19.10   It appears that very few LAs and HAs had a systematic approach to obtaining feedback from victims on their experiences and views of services, and from the comments given, it was not clear whether any of the information obtained was recorded in such a way that it could be shared with other staff members and agencies.

---

[5]   The Home Office is currently preparing guidelines on this issue.

References

Bowling, B and Saulsbury, W, 1993, *The North Plaistow Project: a multi agency approach to racial harassment,* in Tackling Racial Attacks, CSPO, Leicester University.

CATCH (Co-operative and Tenant Controlled Housing), 1994, *Getting Black Tenants Involved: a good practice guide for housing associations and co-operatives,* Vernon Clarke.

Chartered Institute of Housing, 1995 edition, *Housing Management Standards Manual.*

Commission for Racial Equality, 1981, *Racial Harassment on Local Authority Housing Estates: a report prepared by the London Race and Housing Forum.*

Commission for Racial Equality, 1987, *Living in Terror: a report on racial violence and harassment in housing.*

Commission for Racial Equality, 1991, *Code of Practice for Rented Housing.*

Commission for Racial Equality, 1992, *Code of Practice for non Rented (Owner Occupied) Housing.*

Commission for Racial Equality, 1993a, *Housing Associations and Racial Equality: report of a formal investigation into housing associations in Wales, Scotland and England.*

Commission for Racial Equality, 1993b, *Room for All: Tenants' Associations and Racial Equality.*

Commission for Racial Equality, 1995, *Action on Racial Harassment: a guide for multi-agency panels.*

Department of the Environment, 1989, *Tackling Racial Violence and Harassment in Local Authority Housing: a guide to good practice for local authorities.*

Department of the Environment, 1994a, *Racial Incidents in Council Housing: the Local Authority Response,* Anne-Marie Love and Keith Kirby.

Department of the Environment, 1994b, *Moving on, Crossing Divides: A report on policies and procedures for tenants transferring in local authorities and housing associations,* Duncan Maclennan and Helen Kay.

Forbes, D, 1988, *Action on Racial Harassment: Legal Remedies and Local Authorities,* Legal Action Group/London Housing Unit.

Government reply to the third report from the Home Affairs Committee session 1985-86 HC409 Racial Attacks and Harassment. Cm 45, HMSO, 1986.

Home Office Research and Planning Unit Paper 82, 1994, *Racially motivated crime: a British Crime Survey analysis*, N Aye Maung and C Mirrlees-Black.

Home Office Police Research Group, 1995, *Reducing Repeat Racial Victimisation on an East London Housing Estate*, Alice Sampson and Coretta Phillips, Crime Detection and Prevention Series Paper 67.

House of Commons Home Affairs Committee, 1986, *Racial Attacks and Harassment*, HMSO.

House of Commons Home Affairs Committee, 1989, *Racial Attacks and Harassment: report, together with the proceedings of the committee, minutes of evidence and appendices*, HMSO.

House of Commons Home Affairs Committee, 1994, *Racial Attacks and Harassment*, Vols. 1 and 2, HMSO.

Legal Action Group, 1990, *Making the law work against racial harassment: report of the LAG Research Project*.

Lemos Associates, 1993, *Interviewing Perpetrators of Racial Harassment: a guide for housing managers*, Gerard Lemos.

Lemos Associates, 1994, *Eliminating Racial Harassment: a guide to housing policies and procedures*, Richard Seager and Joanna Jeffrey.

Local Authority Housing and Racial Equality Working Party, 1987, Report No. 1: *Racial Harassment*, AMA.

London Research Centre, 1992, *London Housing Statistics, 1991*.

National Federation of Housing Associations, 1982, *Race and Housing: a guide for housing associations*.

National Federation of Housing Associations, 1983, *Race and Housing - Still a Cause for Concern*.

National Federation of Housing Associations, 1989: *Racial Harassment: Policies and Procedures for Housing Associations*.

Racial Attacks Group, 1989, *The Response to Racial Attacks and Harassment: guidance for the statutory agencies*, Home Office.

Racial Attacks Group, 1991, *The Response to Racial Attacks: Sustaining the Momentum*, Home Office.

TPAS (Tenant Participation Advisory Service), 1995, *All Together Now: involving black tenants in housing management*, Joanna Jeffrey and Richard Seager.

Annex 1   Fieldwork

Pilot

The full questionnaire was piloted with ten local authorities and ten housing associations who were known to be working in areas with relatively large ethnic minority populations. These included suburban areas and county towns as well as big cities.

The pilot landlords were asked to complete and return as much of the questionnaire as they could in the short time that was available, and were subsequently contacted on the phone in order to discuss any problems or ambiguities. As a result, a number of minor amendments were made to the questionnaire. The landlords that participated in the pilot were not asked to complete the revised questionnaire, but those that had missed any questions for lack of time were given the opportunity to add to their previous comments. All the questionnaires returned by landlords in the pilot were used in the eventual analysis.

Main stage

The final version of the questionnaire was sent to the remainder of the 598 social landlords (335 local authorities and 263 of the larger housing associations) in October 1994. The local authorities comprised every local housing authority in England that had not transferred its dwelling stock at that date. The housing associations comprised every association with 250 or more general needs properties in England. Recent mergers meant that the potential number of housing association respondents was actually slightly less than 263.

In all cases, questionnaires were addressed to the Director of Housing or equivalent and were accompanied by a covering letter from the DoE. Respondents were asked either to return the short questionnaire if this was appropriate or to send the name and telephone number of the person who would be dealing with the full questionnaire. They were given an initial deadline of seven weeks. Those who had made no response by this time were sent a postal reminder with a new deadline; those who had given a contact for the full questionnaire were telephoned on one or more occasions. All responses received by early December 1994 were coded and keyed for inclusion in the statistical analysis. The latter was done using SPSSx.

The SPSS file from the DoE's 1991 survey was also copied onto the LRC computer so that responses to the full questionnaire could be compared with information provided by the same local authority in 1991. A total of 58 authorities answered the full questionnaire on both occasions, some of whom were participating in multi-agency groups at the time of both surveys.

Choice of questionnaire

It was recognised at the outset that there would be a number of local authorities and housing associations with insufficient experience of dealing with racial harassment to make it feasible for them to complete the whole questionnaire. These landlords were asked instead to indicate whether they were not completing the full questionnaire because they had no experience of racial harassment; no policies for dealing with it; or both.

In the event, quite a large number of landlords (22) completed the full questionnaire even though their responses indicated that they had not recorded *any* cases of racial harassment in the previous year.

It is possible to compare the responses of local authorities with the number of ethnic minority council tenants in the area at the time of the 1991 Census. When this was done, it was found that 80 per cent of those local authorities that had opted for the short questionnaire had fewer then 50 ethnic minority tenants at the Census. With the exception of a district council and two London boroughs (both of whom indicated that they were in the process of reviewing their policies and procedures on racial harassment) the remainder had between 50 and 360 ethnic minority tenants at the Census.

17 of the local authority respondents to the full questionnaire also had fewer than 50 ethnic minority tenants at the Census. The rest ranged up to a metropolitan authority and three London boroughs with more than 11,000 ethnic minority tenants each.

Although it is not possible to make the same check on housing associations using Census data, these findings do suggest that the vast majority of landlords acted conscientiously in their choice of questionnaire.

Response rates

The response by early December, when questionnaires were keyed onto computer, was as follows:

	LAs	%	HAs	%	Total	%
Completed full questionnaire	93	28	97	37	190	32
Completed short questionnaire	202	60	125	48	327	55
No response	39	12	39	15	78	13
Refused	1	–	2	1	3	1
Total (100%)	335		263		598	

Although not all responses were received in time to be included in the statistical analysis, any views and comments were taken into account in the qualitative analysis. The final response rates are shown below:

	LAs	%	HAs	%	Total	%
Completed full questionnaire	103	31	100	38	203	34
Completed short questionnaire	205	63	128	49	333	56
No response	26	8	33	13	59	10
Refused	1	-	2	1	3	1
Total (100%)	335		263		598	

An analysis of LA returns by DoE region shows that once late returns had been allowed for (mainly London and the West Midlands) the overall response rate was similar throughout the country, although there was variation in the ratio of full to short questionnaires.

LA response rates by region (excluding late returns)

	Eligible LAs	Full Q	Short Q	% response
Greater London	32	20	4	75
North	23	5	15	87
Yorkshire & Humberside	24	9	14	96
East Midlands	40	10	29	98
Eastern	42	9	26	83
South East	55	13	39	95
South West	43	6	30	86
West Midlands	34	6	20	76
North West	42	15	24	93
Total	335	93	202	88

LA response rates by region (including late returns)

	Eligible LAs	Full Q	Short Q	% response
Greater London	32	25	4	91
North	23	5	16	91
Yorkshire & Humber	24	9	14	96
East Mids	40	10	29	98
Eastern	42	10	28	90
South East	55	13	39	95
South West	43	6	30	86
West Mids	34	9	20	85
North West	42	16	24	95
Total	335	103	205	92

The eventual response rate from LAs did not vary by type of authority, but a much higher proportion of respondents in the metropolitan areas opted for the full questionnaire.

LA response rates by type of authority (excluding late returns)

	Eligible LAs	Full Q	Short Q	% response
Greater London	32	20	4	75
Other mets	36	21	8	81
Non mets	267	52	190	91

LA response rates by type of authority (including late returns)				
	Eligible LAs	Full Q	Short Q	% response
Greater London	32	25	4	91
Other mets	36	24	9	92
Non mets	267	54	192	92

Some housing associations operate over a very wide geographical area and some of these have a highly devolved regional structure. Since the incidence of racial harassment and the existence of multi-agency groups and other types of response vary in different parts of the country, it can be difficult to distil the experience of a national association onto a single questionnaire. In order to overcome this problem, those associations which felt they were in this position were given the option of completing more than one questionnaire. As a result, four associations completed 11 questionnaires between them. Since these extra respondents would have qualified under the criterion for the survey as associations in their own right (ie more than 250 general needs properties) they were treated as such in the analysis. This brought the number of full housing association questionnaires included in the analysis to 104 – the number that appears in most of the tables in the report.

Racial incidents reported to social housing landlords

A survey of local housing authorities and housing associations for the Department of the Environment

PLEASE RETURN THIS PAGE IMMEDIATELY USING THE SMALL REPLY-PAID ENVELOPE

Name of local authority or housing association _____

(329-331)

EITHER

This questionnaire is being dealt with by:

Name _____

Job title _____

Address _____

_____

Tel _____

OR

We are not completing this questionnaire because (please tick one box only)

We have little or no experience of racial harassment in our dwelling stock and have not developed policies and procedures in this area ☐ 1

We have policies and procedures but very little experience of racial harassment ☐ 2

We are aware of some incidents of racial harassment in the stock but do not yet have policies and procedures to deal with it ☐ 3

Other reason (please give details) ☐ 4

(332)

HOUSING ASSOCIATIONS - please tick here if you would like some or all of the questionnaire to be answered at a local or regional level (we will phone you to make arrangements). ☐ (333)

London Research Centre

Racial incidents reported to social housing landlords

A survey of local housing authorities and housing associations for the Department of the Environment

Name of local authority or housing association _____

Questionnaire completed by:

Name _____

Job title _____

Address _____

_____

Tel _____

Nearly all the questions ask you to tick one or more boxes, or to write comments in the space provided. Please indicate when you do not know the answer, or when the question does not apply to your organisation. Otherwise we have no way of knowing whether you missed a question by mistake.

If you wish to provide additional information on a separate sheet of paper, please indicate the question number to which your comments apply.

Housing associations - the level of racial harassment may vary considerably in different parts of the country. If you feel it would also be appropriate for questionnaires to be completed by any of your local/regional offices, we would be pleased to make arrangements with you.

Please return the completed questionnaire by **1 November** using the large reply paid envelope provided. If you have any queries, please telephone **Yvonne Dhooge** on 071 627 9640

Social Surveys Section
London Research Centre
81 Black Prince Road
London
SE1 7SZ

Tel 071 627 9640

Thank you for completing the questionnaire

London Research Centre

POLICY BACKGROUND

Please indicate below those situations for which your organisation has written policies and procedures when dealing with racial attacks and harassment.

Please tick all that apply

Secure/assured tenancies in your own stock	☐ (4)
Shared ownership tenancies	☐ (5)
RTB or other leaseholders	☐ (6)
Households in hostels, short life or B&B accommodation	☐ (7)
Properties leased from the private sector (eg PSL, HAMA , HAL)	☐ (8)
LAs only Any local residents living in the private sector (owning or renting)	☐ (9)
OR No policy in any of these situations	☐ (10)

Does your organisation keep the following ethnic records?

Please tick all that apply

Ethnic origin of new applicants for housing	☐ (11)
Ethnic origin of all existing tenants	☐ (12)
Ethnic origin of victims of racial harassment	☐ (13)
OR None of these records kept	☐ (14)

RACIAL INCIDENTS

This question relates to **incidents** of racial violence or harassment reported to your organisation by people in the following tenure categories in 1993 (calendar year) **or** 1993/4 (financial year). Please try to give data on incidents rather than households. If your data *do* relate to households, tick this box ☐   (15)

Tick one box in each column Number of incidents	Secure or assured tenants	Hostels short life or B&B	Properties leased from private sector (eg PSL, HAMA, HAL)	Lease holders (eg RTB)	Shared owners	
None	☐ 01	☐ 01	☐ 01	☐ 01	☐ 01	(16-17)
1-9	☐ 02	☐ 02	☐ 02	☐ 02	☐ 02	
10-19	☐ 03	☐ 03	☐ 03	☐ 03	☐ 03	(18-19)
20-49	☐ 04	☐ 04	☐ 04	☐ 04	☐ 04	
50-99	☐ 05	☐ 05	☐ 05	☐ 05	☐ 05	(20-21)
100-199	☐ 06	☐ 06	☐ 06	☐ 06	☐ 06	
200-299	☐ 07	☐ 07	☐ 07	☐ 07	☐ 07	(22-23)
300 or more	☐ 08	☐ 08	☐ 08	☐ 08	☐ 08	
Records not kept	☐ 09	☐ 09	☐ 09	☐ 09	☐ 09	(24-25)
Not involved in this type of accommodation	☐ 97	☐ 97	☐ 97	☐ 97	☐ 97	

4 Would any of the following usually be informed (with the victim's consent) about **individual** racial attacks on the person reported to your organisation?

Please tick all that apply

Senior staff/management team	☐	(26)
Housing Committee (if LA) or Management Ctee (if HA)	☐	(27)
Ward councillors	☐	(28)
Police	☐	(29)
Local race equality council	☐	(30)
Local tenants'/residents' association	☐	(31)
Tenant consultative group	☐	(32)
Local authority (or other depts if you are an LA)	☐	(33)
Local monitoring group/community organisation	☐	(34)
Victim support scheme	☐	(35)
Multi agency group	☐	(36)
OR None of the above	☐	(37)

5 Do any of the following receive regular reports (at least once a year) about the **level** of racial attacks and harassment reported to your organisation?

Please tick all that apply

Senior staff/management team	☐	(38)
Housing Committee (if LA) or Management Ctee (if HA)	☐	(39)
Police	☐	(40)
Local race equality council	☐	(41)
Local tenants'/residents' associations	☐	(42)
Tenant consultative group	☐	(43)
Local authority (or other depts if you are an LA)	☐	(44)
(Other) housing associations operating in the area	☐	(45)
Local monitoring group/community organisation	☐	(46)
Victim support scheme	☐	(47)
Multi agency group	☐	(48)
OR None of the above	☐	(49)

6 Does providing information to any of the agencies in Q4 or Q5 present any problems for your organisation? (Exclude the police, who are covered in a later question)

1 ☐ Yes - please give details below   2 ☐ No   7 ☐ Does not apply

(50)

(51-52)

(53-54)

(55-56)

a Does your organisation **receive** information about incidents of racial violence and harassment from any of the following? This question applies both to individual incidents affecting your tenants/residents (as victims or perpetrators) and monitoring information on the general level of harassment in the area.

Please tick all that apply	Individual incidents	Statistical monitoring	
Local authority/other LA depts	☐	☐	(57-58)
Housing associations/other HAs	☐	☐	(59-60)
Police	☐	☐	(61-62)
Local race equality council	☐	☐	(63-64)
TAs/residents' associations	☐	☐	(65-66)
Local monitoring group/community organisation	☐	☐	(67-68)
Victim support scheme	☐	☐	(69-70)
Multi agency group	☐	☐	(71-72)
OR None of the above	☐	☐	(73-74)

If you have ticked any of the above, please comment below on the usefulness of the information you receive from each source. For example, is it accurate, timely, and in a form that enables you to act upon it?

Source	Usefulness of data	
		(75-78)
		(79-82)
		(83-86)
		(87-90)

For any agencies that were **not** ticked above, please list those from whom you would **like** to receive information, whether this has ever been requested, and the outcome of your request.

Source	Whether requested		Outcome of request	
	(1) Yes	(2) No		
				(91-93)
				(94-96)
				(97-99)
				(100-102)

8 Has your organisation experienced any particular obstacles to sharing information on racial incidents with the local police?

1 ☐ Yes - please give details below   2 ☐ No - please go to Q9   8 ☐ Don't know - please go to Q9

(103)

A Giving information to the police

(104-105)

(106-107)

(108-109)

B Receiving information from the police

(110-111)

(112-113)

(114-115)

9 Please comment below if you have examples of good practice in the exchange of information with any of the agencies in Q7, or ways in which obstacles to communication have been overcome.

(116-117)

(118-119)

(120-121)

PREVENTION

10 Does your organisation try to prevent racial violence and harassment in any of the following ways?

Please tick all that apply

Publicising racial violence and harassment policy to tenants	☐	(122)
Clause in tenancy agreement specifically forbidding harassment	☐	(123)
Requiring tenants' associations to adopt anti-racial violence and harassment policies	☐	(124)
Community development work on estates	☐	(125)
Advising tenants of the steps they should take in the event of encountering racial harassment	☐	(126)
Other - please give details below	☐	(127)
OR None of the above	☐	(128)

(129)

(130)

ACTION AGAINST PERPETRATORS

11 Has your organisation dealt with perpetrators of racial violence and harassment in any of the following ways?

Please tick all that apply

Issuing notices of seeking possession (NOSPs) (if yes, please also answer Q12)	☐	(131)
Interviewing and warning known perpetrators	☐	(132)
Writing to known perpetrators warning them of the consequences	☐	(133)
Taking out an injunction	☐	(134)
Warning letters to all tenants when perpetrators are not known	☐	(135)
Other - please give details below	☐	(136)
OR None of the above	☐	(137)

12 If you issue NOSPs, please provide the information below. Otherwise, please go to Q14.

Number of NOSPs issued in 1993 or 1993/4 (financial year)	_____	(140-142)
Number of above taken to court	_____	(143-144)
Number taken to court and granted immediate possession	_____	(145-146)
Number taken to court and granted suspended possession	_____	(147-148)
Number evicted	_____	(149-150)
Number of cases not proven	_____	(151-152)
Number where the outcome is not yet known	_____	(153-154)

13 If you have taken NOSP cases to court (whether in 1993/94 or previously) have you found the courts to be generally understanding of the need to deal with racial attacks and harassment? Please comment in the space below.

(155-156)

(157-158)

(159-160)

London Research Centre

VICTIM SUPPORT

14 Do any of the following statements apply to your organisation?

Please tick all that apply

Repairs to the homes of victims carried out within a target time ☐ (161)

Witness support or protection scheme in operation ☐ (162)

Complaints procedure in operation when victims do not feel they have ☐ (163)

received adequate support

Victim support packs provided ☐ (164)

OR None of the above ☐ (165)

COMMUNICATION WITH VICTIMS

15 Does your LA/HA inform victims of racial incidents about the systems and organisations in place to support and advise them?

1 ☐ Yes - please give examples of how this is done   2 ☐ No - please go to Q16   (166)

(167-168)

(169-170)

(171-172)

16 To your knowledge, have any local surveys been undertaken of victims of racial incidents?

1 ☐ Yes   2 ☐ No - please go to Q19   (173)

If yes, who commissioned or undertook this survey?

Please tick all that apply

Local authority housing dept ☐ (174)

Local authority - other dept ☐ (175)

Local race equality council ☐ (176)

Victim support scheme ☐ (177)

Tenants' group ☐ (178)

Voluntary/community group ☐ (179)

Housing association ☐ (180)

Police ☐ (181)

Health authority ☐ (182)

Other - please specify below ☐ (183)

(184)

PLEASE SEND DETAILS OF THE SURVEY IF POSSIBLE (date, methodology, summary of findings)

7 Has your organisation discussed the findings of the survey?

1 ☐ Yes   2 ☐ No

8 Have the findings affected your work in this area?

1 ☐ Yes - please explain below how they have affected your work   2 ☐ No - please go to Q19

9 Has your organisation taken any steps other than surveys to get feedback from victims of racial incidents on:

A Their experience of racial harassment?

1 ☐ Yes - please give details below   2 ☐ No - please go to Q19B

B Their perceptions of the way in which incidents have been dealt with by agencies such as yourselves?

1 ☐ Yes - please give details below   2 ☐ No - please go to Q20

] Do you think it would be helpful to have written guidance on how to carry out local surveys of victims of racial harassment?

1 ☐ Yes   2 ☐ No - please go to Q21

If yes, please tick all that apply

How to measure the scale and nature of the problem ☐

How to find out about the support needs of victims ☐

How to evaluate the service currently provided to victims ☐

Other - please specify below ☐

(185)

(186)

(187-188)

(189-190)

(191-192)

(193)

(194-195)

(196-197)

(198-199)

(200)

(201-202)

(203-204)

(205-206)

(207)

(208)

(209)

(210)

(211)

(212)

(213)

21 Please comment below if you have examples of good practice in communicating with victims, or ways in which obstacles to communication have been overcome.

(214-215)

(216-217)

(218-219)

(220-221)

(222-223)

MULTI AGENCY APPROACH

22 Is there a multi-agency group on racial violence and harassment in your area?

1 ☐ Yes   2 ☐ No - please go to Q31   8 ☐ Don't know - please go to Q31

(224)

23 What is the status of the group?

Please tick one box only

Informal liaison group	☐ 1	(225)
Formally constituted group	☐ 2	(226)
Other - please give details below	☐ 3	(227)

(228)

24 Who represents your organisation?

Please tick all that apply

Elected members (LAs) or Committee members (HAs)	☐	(229)
Chief officers	☐	(230)
Senior staff	☐	(231)
First line managers	☐	(232)
Front line staff	☐	(233)
Others - please give details below	☐	(234)

(235)

(236)

25 Which of the following agencies are represented?

Please tick all that apply

LA depts - *Housing*	☐ (237)
- *Chief Executives*	☐ (238)
- *Education*	☐ (239)
- *Youth Service*	☐ (240)
- *Social Services*	☐ (241)
- *Legal*	☐ (242)
Police	☐ (243)
Race equality council	☐ (244)
Victim support scheme	☐ (245)
Ethnic minority organisations	☐ (246)
Tenants/residents groups	☐ (247)
Other voluntary/community groups	☐ (248)
Health authority	☐ (249)
Other - please give details below	☐ (250)
	(251)
	(252)

What types of activity is the group involved in ?

Please tick all that apply

Exchange of information about individual cases	☐ (253)
Exchange of information about general trends	☐ (254)
Coordinated action against perpetrators	☐ (255)
Preventative work/publicity campaigns	☐ (256)
Victim support	☐ (257)
Other - please give details below	☐ (258)
	(259)
	(260)

What have been the benefits of working together in a multi agency group?

Please tick all that apply

No benefits	☐ (261)
Increased understanding between agencies	☐ (262)
Better coordination	☐ (263)
Adoption of common definitions	☐ (264)
Improvements in recording/reporting practice	☐ (265)
More cases coming to light	☐ (266)

Please do not write in this space

28 Do you think cases are being tackled more effectively because of multi-agency working?

1 ☐ Yes   2 ☐ No

Please give reasons for your answer

(267)

(268-269)

(270-271)

(272-273)

29 Are there any problems or obstacles to sharing information in the context of a multi-agency group?

1 ☐ Yes - please give details below   2 ☐ No - please go to Q30

(274)

A Getting information

(275-276)

(277-278)

(279-280)

B Giving information

(281-282)

(283-284)

(285-286)

30 What have been the other problems of working together in the multi agency group? .

Please tick all that apply

No problems	☐	(287)
Problems with the definition of racial harassment	☐	(288)
Lack of cooperation or commitment from some agencies	☐	(289)
Problems in agreeing the role that each agency should play	☐	(290)
Lack of resources	☐	(291)
Tensions between agencies on issues other than racial violence or harassment	☐	(292)
Other - please give details below	☐	(293)

(294)

(295)

London Research Centre

SUMMING UP

1 Please give examples of any successes your organisation has had in dealing with **victims** of racial harassment.

A Acting alone

B Acting in conjunction with other agencies

2 Please give examples of any successes your organisation has had in dealing with **perpetrators** of racial harassment.

A Acting alone

B Acting in conjunction with other agencies

Please do not write in this space

(296-297)

(298-299)

(300-301)

(302-303)

(304-305)

(306-307)

(308-309)

(310-311)

(312-313)

(314-315)

(316-317)

(318-319)

33 Has your local authority/housing association communicated information about these successful cases to tenants or other members of the public?

1 ☐ Yes   2 ☐ No - please go to Q34   7 ☐ Does not apply - please go to Q34

If yes - what form did this take?

Has this had any impact?

1 ☐ Yes - please give details below   2 ☐ No - please go to Q34

34 Please add any other relevant information.

Thank you for answering the questionnaire. Please remember to complete the details on the first page and return in the reply paid envelope.

London Research Centre

Printed in the United Kingdom for HMSO.
Dd.301608, C12, 6/96, 3396/4, 5673, 354794.